CW00400993

# English for
# **Socializing**

## EXPRESS SERIES

Sylee Gore & David Gordon Smith

**OXFORD**
UNIVERSITY PRESS

# OXFORD
UNIVERSITY PRESS

Great Clarendon Street, Oxford OX2 6DP

Oxford University Press is a department of the University of Oxford.
It furthers the University's objective of excellence in research, scholarship,
and education by publishing worldwide in

Oxford  New York

Auckland  Cape Town  Dar es Salaam  Hong Kong  Karachi
Kuala Lumpur  Madrid  Melbourne  Mexico City  Nairobi
New Delhi  Shanghai  Taipei  Toronto

With offices in

Argentina  Austria  Brazil  Chile  Czech Republic  France  Greece
Guatemala  Hungary  Italy  Japan  Poland  Portugal  Singapore
South Korea  Switzerland  Thailand  Turkey  Ukraine  Vietnam

OXFORD and OXFORD ENGLISH are registered trade marks of
Oxford University Press in the UK and in certain other countries

© Oxford University Press 2007

Adapted from *English for Small Talk & Socializing*
by Sylee Gore and David Gordon Smith
© Cornelscn Verlag GmbH & Co. OHG, Berlin 2006
The moral rights of the author have been asserted
Database right Oxford University Press (maker)

First published 2007
2011  2010  2009  2008  2007
10  9  8  7  6  5  4  3  2  1

**No unauthorized photocopying**

All rights reserved. No part of this publication may be reproduced,
stored in a retrieval system, or transmitted, in any form or by any
means, without the prior permission in writing of Oxford University
Press, or as expressly permitted by law, or under terms agreed with the
appropriate reprographics rights organization. Enquiries concerning
reproduction outside the scope of the above should be sent to the
ELT Rights Department, Oxford University Press, at the address above

You must not circulate this book in any other binding or cover
and you must impose this same condition on any acquirer

Any websites referred to in this publication are in the public domain
and their addresses are provided by Oxford University Press for
information only. Oxford University Press disclaims any responsibility
for the content

ISBN: 978 0 19 457940 7

Printed in China

ACKNOWLEDGEMENTS

*Prepared for OUP by Starfish Design Editorial and Project Management Ltd*

*Cartoons by*: Philip Burrows and Stephen May

*Photo credits*: istock photo library and inmagine

*Cover images courtesy of*: Getty Images (main image/Romilly Lockyer/
Image Bank) and Punchstock (bottom left/Digital Vision; top left/
Photodisc)

## M-ROM  MultiROM

**English for Socializing** is accompanied by a MultiROM which
has a number of features.

**Interactive exercises** to practise useful phrases, vocabulary,
and communication through your computer.

**Listening extracts**. These are in enhanced audio format that
can be played on a conventional CD-player or through the
audio player on your computer.

If you have any problems, please check the technical support
section of the readme file on the MultiROM.

# Contents

# About the book

**English for Socializing** is for people who want to be able to build good relationships with international clients and colleagues. Whether you are at a business dinner, an exhibition stand, showing a visitor around your company, or attending an event after work – you need to be able make conversation in an appropriate and confident way in order to establish and maintain successful business relationships. **English for Socializing** presents all the essential expressions and conversation techniques that will enable you to socialize and make business contacts in English.

The six units of **English for Socializing** present realistic relationship-building situations. There are numerous interesting, varied, and well-structured exercises and activities that allow you to practise conversational techniques and strategies. The **Partner Files** at the back of the book provide role-play exercises which practise the language you have learnt in the unit. **English for Socializing** also addresses intercultural issues and soft skills.

Every unit begins with a **Starter** to introduce the topic. These speaking activities are designed to raise awareness of the potential difficulties that you may face when you want to establish a good business relationship, exchange pleasantries, or simply chat with ease. The units end with **Output**, which consists of reading texts to extend the unit topic or offer further useful tips, and also provides opportunities for discussion. When you have finished all the units, you can **Test yourself!** with a fun crossword at the back of the book.

The **MultiROM** contains all the **Listening extracts** from the book. These can be played through the audio player on your computer, or through a conventional CD-player. In order to give yourself extra listening practice, listen to it in your car or download it to your MP3-player and listen when you are out and about. The **Interactive exercises** let you review by doing exercises that cover the essential language from the book on you computer, this will be particularly valuable if you are using the book for self-study.

At the back of **English for Socializing** there is an **Answer key** so that you can check your answers independently. There is also an **A–Z word list**, the **Transcripts** of the listening extracts, and a **Useful phrases and vocabulary** list that you can refer to when preparing to speak to customers and colleagues. You will also find **Vocabulary banks** in this section that you can use to make small talk on a variety of topics.

# 1 Making contact

STARTER

**First look at some of the activities involved in socializing. Can you add anything?**

making small talk at a meeting

introducing visitors

showing a visitor around your town or city

chatting during a coffee break

greeting a visitor

taking a visitor out to lunch or dinner

networking at a trade fair or conference

**Now work with a partner to ask and answer the following questions.**

1   When and where do you need to socialize in English?
2   Who do you speak to? Are they native or non-native English speakers? Who do you find easier to understand?
3   What topics do you talk about? What topics are 'taboo' in your culture?
4   What do you find difficult about socializing in English? What do you enjoy?
5   How do you break the ice?

**1** Emails are often used to make arrangements for company visits. Look at the three emails below. Which email is the most formal? How can you tell?

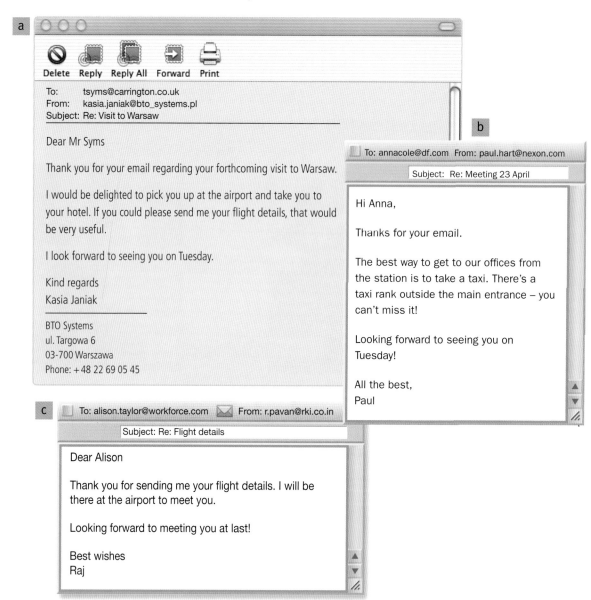

**a**

Delete Reply Reply All Forward Print

To: tsyms@carrington.co.uk
From: kasia.janiak@bto_systems.pl
Subject: Re: Visit to Warsaw

Dear Mr Syms

Thank you for your email regarding your forthcoming visit to Warsaw.

I would be delighted to pick you up at the airport and take you to your hotel. If you could please send me your flight details, that would be very useful.

I look forward to seeing you on Tuesday.

Kind regards
Kasia Janiak

BTO Systems
ul. Targowa 6
03-700 Warszawa
Phone: + 48 22 69 05 45

**b**

To: annacole@df.com From: paul.hart@nexon.com

Subject: Re: Meeting 23 April

Hi Anna,

Thanks for your email.

The best way to get to our offices from the station is to take a taxi. There's a taxi rank outside the main entrance – you can't miss it!

Looking forward to seeing you on Tuesday!

All the best,
Paul

**c**

To: alison.taylor@workforce.com From: r.pavan@rki.co.in

Subject: Re: Flight details

Dear Alison

Thank you for sending me your flight details. I will be there at the airport to meet you.

Looking forward to meeting you at last!

Best wishes
Raj

**AUDIO**
2–4

**2** You will hear three conversations about people meeting visitors. First match the conversations to the emails above.

Conversation    Email

1               ☐

2               ☐

3               ☐

**AUDIO**
2–4

**Now listen again and complete the chart.**

|  | Conversation 1 | Conversation 2 | Conversation 3 |
|---|---|---|---|
| 1 Have the speakers met before? |  |  |  |
| 2 Is the conversation formal or informal? |  |  |  |
| 3 Where are they meeting? |  |  |  |
| 4 What problems did the visitors have during the journey? |  |  |  |
| 5 What are they doing next? |  |  |  |

**3** **Complete the sentences from the dialogues. Listen again if necessary.**

1  You _____ be Raj.

2  It's great to _____ meet you in _____ after all our phone calls and emails.

3  I _____ you haven't been _____ long.

4  It's a _____ to meet you.

5  How was your _____?

6  Hi, Paul, good to _____ you _____.

7  Sorry to keep you _____.

8  Can I _____ you with your _____?

9  Would you _____ taking this?

**Which sentences above are used to:**

a   welcome or greet the visitor? _____

b   talk about the journey? _____

c   offer (or ask for) help with something? _____

d   apologize for a delay? _____

---

**ATTITUDES TO TIME**

Note how both Alison and Anna apologize for being late. Different cultures have different attitudes to time, meaning that what counts as 'late' varies from country to country. In Britain and the US you can usually arrive up to 15 minutes after the agreed time without being 'late'. In other countries, such as Portugal, up to 40 minutes after the agreed time is often acceptable.

What is the attitude in your country? What is considered 'late' for a business meeting or a dinner appointment?

---

**4** **Match the questions with the answers. Some questions have more than one answer.**

1 Can I help you with your bags?
2 Would you mind taking this?
3 How was your flight?
4 How was your journey?

5 How was the drive?
6 Is there a toilet around here?
7 Is there a café where we could sit down?
8 Where are we going from here?

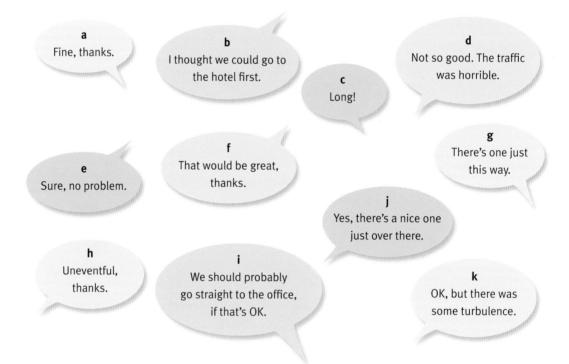

**a**
Fine, thanks.

**b**
I thought we could go to the hotel first.

**c**
Long!

**d**
Not so good. The traffic was horrible.

**g**
There's one just this way.

**e**
Sure, no problem.

**f**
That would be great, thanks.

**j**
Yes, there's a nice one just over there.

**h**
Uneventful, thanks.

**i**
We should probably go straight to the office, if that's OK.

**k**
OK, but there was some turbulence.

---

**TOILET OR RESTROOM?**

British people talk about the *toilet* or *loo*, which is more informal. *WC* [ˌdʌblju: ˈsi:] is now old-fashioned.
Using the word *toilet* is not polite in American English, however! When talking to Americans, say *restroom* or *bathroom*.

**5** **Work with a partner. Use the profiles in the Partner Files to practise meeting visitors. Try to use phrases from the Language Box below.**

PARTNER FILES ➤ Partner A File 1, p. 60
Partner B File 1, p. 62

---

**MEETING VISITORS ON ARRIVAL**

**Greetings**
Nice/Good/Great to see you again.
  *(when you know sb already)*
Nice/Good/Great to meet you (at last).
  *(when you are meeting sb for the first time)*

**Apologizing for a delay**
I hope you haven't been waiting long.
Sorry to keep you waiting.

**Asking about the journey**
How was the/your flight/journey?
How was the drive? (AmE) *(if sb comes by car)*

Try to avoid these common mistakes:
~~Nice to meet you again.~~    Nice to **see** you again.
~~How was your fly?~~    How was your **flight**?
~~I take you to your hotel.~~    **I'll** take you to your hotel.

**Offering and asking for help**
Can I help you with your bags?
Let me get/take that for you.
Would you mind taking this?

**The next step**
I'd just like to wash my hands.
Is there a toilet (BrE)/restroom (AmE) around here?
Is there a café where we could sit down/get
  something to drink?
Where are we going now?

---

**6** **Kasia Janiak is accompanying Mr Syms from the airport to his hotel. Look at the dialogue below and try to complete the gaps. What is the topic of their conversation?**

| | |
|---|---|
| *Mr Syms* | I can't believe it's so _s_____ [1] here. It makes a nice change from England! |
| *Kasia* | How was the _w_____ [2] when you left? |
| *Mr Syms* | It was _r_____ [3], as usual! This summer has been _t_____ [4]. |
| *Kasia* | Well, we've been very _l_____ [5] here. The last couple of weeks have been very _w_____ [6]. |
| *Mr Syms* | Do you normally get good summers here? |
| *Kasia* | It depends. Usually we get at least a few _h_____ [7] days, but sometimes it rains a lot. |
| *Mr Syms* | I imagine the winters here must be pretty _c_____ [8]. |
| *Kasia* | Oh yes. Sometimes it goes _d_____ [9] to minus 15. |
| *Mr Syms* | Well, at least it never gets that cold in England. The winter there is usually just grey and _w_____ [10]. It can be quite depressing! |
| *Kasia* | Ugh! Well, I'm glad the weather is nice for your visit here … |

**AUDIO**
🔊
5

**Listen to the conversation and check your answers.**

**7** **The weather is one of the most popular small-talk topics. It is a topic everybody can talk about. Put the words below into the right categories.**

cloudy • cold • damp • drizzling • freezing • grey • hazy • humid • mild • overcast • pouring • rainy • roasting • sunny • warm

| words describing temperature | words describing the sky | words to do with water |
|---|---|---|
| cold | cloudy | damp |
| | | |
| | | |
| | | |

**Now use words from the table to complete these sentences.**

It's _____ today.

It was _____ yesterday morning.

It was _____ yesterday evening.

The weather during my last business trip (or holiday) was _____ .

AUDIO  6

**8** **Mr Syms and Ms Janiak are talking about their plans. Listen and complete Ms Janiak's diary.**

12 AUGUST

9.00

10.00

11.00  11:40 Mr Syms arrives at
Warsaw airport, flight BA120

12.00  12 (approx)
– Il Casolare

13.00

14.00

15.00

12 AUGUST

16.00

17.00

18.00

19.00

20.00

21.00

22.00

Activities

Datafile

Contacts

AUDIO

6

**9** **Listen again and complete the sentences from the dialogue.**

1 It's _____ now. We'll be _____ in five minutes.

2 I thought you might like to _____ your hotel first and _____
your things.

3 Then we _____ a spot of lunch. There's a nice Italian place _____
your hotel.

4 After that we _____ to the office.

5 We _____ with the sales team at two, as you know.

6 At four we _____ the
production plant.

7 That _____ an hour.

8 Then perhaps you _____ a taxi
back to your hotel and _____ for
a bit.

9 I _____ again at
about seven for dinner.

10 It _____ really good.
We _____ to this fantastic
French restaurant.

> I've scheduled your argument
> with the marketing
> director for 3.30.

---

**TALKING ABOUT PLANS**

There are many ways to talk about future plans in English, and often you can say the same thing in different ways. Here are some ways to talk about plans:

- using modals verbs such as *can*, *could*, *might*, *should*, etc:
*I thought you might like to check into your hotel first.*
*Then we can go to the office.*
*That should only take an hour.*

- using the present tense:
*We have the meeting with the sales team at two.*
*It's the big company dinner tonight.*

- using *will*:
*I'll pick you up again at about seven for dinner.*

- using *going to*:
*At four we're going to visit the production plant.*
*After that we're going to this fantastic French restaurant.*

**10** Work with a partner to make a dialogue. Person A: you are the host. You are dropping B off at his/her hotel. Person B: you are the visitor.

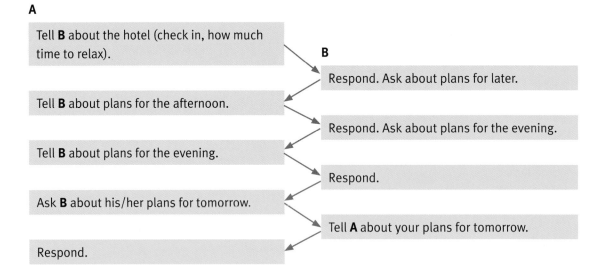

**A**

Tell **B** about the hotel (check in, how much time to relax).

**B**

Respond. Ask about plans for later.

Tell **B** about plans for the afternoon.

Respond. Ask about plans for the evening.

Tell **B** about plans for the evening.

Respond.

Ask **B** about his/her plans for tomorrow.

Tell **A** about your plans for tomorrow.

Respond.

**11** Complete the crossword. Then rearrange the letters in the orange squares to find the mystery phrase.

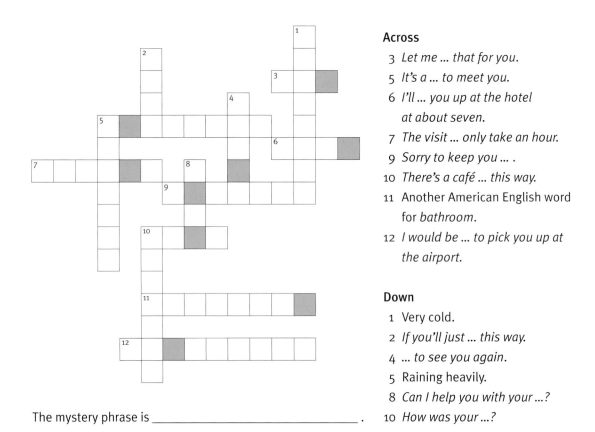

**Across**

3 *Let me … that for you.*
5 *It's a … to meet you.*
6 *I'll … you up at the hotel at about seven.*
7 *The visit … only take an hour.*
9 *Sorry to keep you … .*
10 *There's a café … this way.*
11 Another American English word for *bathroom*.
12 *I would be … to pick you up at the airport.*

**Down**

1 Very cold.
2 *If you'll just … this way.*
4 *… to see you again.*
5 Raining heavily.
8 *Can I help you with your …?*
10 *How was your …?*

The mystery phrase is _____ .

OUTPUT **Read the article and discuss the questions which follow.**

# Why it's important to mix business with pleasure

### Sarah Smith

*Socializing with your business contacts isn't just for fun – it can also make doing business a lot easier. How many business deals have been closed not in the boardroom, but in a restaurant or bar?*
*Not everybody agrees with this, though. We look at some of the most common myths about socializing.*

### Myth #1: 'I don't need to socialize with my business contacts.'

You work long hours in the office and work hard all day long. You don't need to go to dinner with your business contacts as well, right? Wrong!

Ever since people first began trading and making deals, there has never been business without socializing. In many cultures the socializing *is* the business – people only do business with their friends, and if you're not friends already you have to become friends before you can make a deal. Even in the more 'business-like' West, socializing is still extremely important. In fact, in some countries, such as Britain, *not* socializing with business contacts is seen as very impolite and could damage your relationship.

### Myth #2: 'Small talk is superficial.'

Many people find typical British and American small-talk topics, like the weather or sport, very superficial. Well, maybe saying it's a nice day isn't as deep as discussing philosophy. But that's not the point. This kind of small talk is a social ritual known as 'phatic' communication, where what's important is not what you say, but the fact you are talking to a particular person and keeping that relationship going.

Also, small talk doesn't always have to be about the weather, but you need to start somewhere! Building a relationship takes time. 'Superficial' small-talk topics give you a chance to start a conversation with someone. If it goes well, you can talk about 'deeper' things later.

### Myth #3: 'When British and American people ask "How are you?" they don't mean it.'

Yes and no. It's true that when most native speakers ask someone 'How are you?' they expect to hear an answer like 'Fine, thanks' or 'Not bad'. They don't really want to hear about your problems and will be surprised (and even embarrassed) if you start talking about how you really feel.

However, saying that you're fine even if you're not, doesn't need to be a bad thing. Do you really want to tell everyone you meet about your back problem or the fact that your husband has just lost his job?

But sometimes 'How are you?' can also be a real question requiring a real answer. If you're talking to someone you know well, you can tell them the truth when they ask how you are, even if you're not feeling so good. After all, talking about problems honestly can be a good way to build a relationship.

### Myth #4: 'English speakers behave like they're your friend, but they're not.'

In the UK and the US, it's important to behave as if everyone is your friend. But this doesn't mean they're insincere. What's important is to read between the lines. Is the person just being polite, or do they really mean it? If someone says 'Let's meet up next time you're in London', they are probably just being polite. But if they give you their phone number and tell you to call them, then they really mean it. Remember: sometimes people are nice to you because they like you! ∎

OVER TO YOU

- What are your experiences with socializing with people from other cultures? What differences (and similarities) have you experienced?
- How important is it to tell the truth in social situations?
- In what ways do you try to build a relationship with a new business contact?

# 2 Welcoming visitors

Complete the quiz on company visitors.

## When welcoming a visitor to your company, how important is it to ...

| | very important | somewhat important | not important | it depends |
|---|---|---|---|---|
| → find out about your visitor's company? | ☐ | ☐ | ☐ | ☐ |
| → find out about your visitor's country and culture? | ☐ | ☐ | ☐ | ☐ |
| → be at the reception when your visitor arrives? | ☐ | ☐ | ☐ | ☐ |
| → make sure the receptionist knows how to pronounce your visitor's name? | ☐ | ☐ | ☐ | ☐ |
| → give your visitor a tour of the office? | ☐ | ☐ | ☐ | ☐ |
| → introduce your visitor to other members of the team? | ☐ | ☐ | ☐ | ☐ |
| → offer your visitor something to eat and drink? | ☐ | ☐ | ☐ | ☐ |
| → show your visitor where the toilets are? | ☐ | ☐ | ☐ | ☐ |

Now discuss your answers with a partner. How often do people visit your company? Where are your visitors from? What difficulties do you have socializing with visitors to your company?

AUDIO
7

1 José María Molinero is meeting a visitor. Listen to the conversation and tick the topics they talk about.

the journey ☐

the weather ☐

the hotel ☐

sport ☐

the offices ☐

the company ☐

AUDIO

7

**Now listen again and answer these questions.**

1 What is the visitor's name? _____

2 Have the two met before? _____

3 Why does José María take the visitor into his office? _____

4 How long has the company been in its current location? _____

5 What does the visitor like about the building? _____

6 When was Salas Design founded? _____

7 How many people work at the company? _____

8 What does the visitor want to drink? _____

---

### USING FIRST NAMES

In general, Britons and Americans prefer to use first names rather than surnames. Colleagues, in particular, nearly always use first names with each other. One exception, however, is when someone of 'low status' is talking to someone of 'high status'. For example, a secretary might call the company CEO *Ms Phillips* and the CEO would call the secretary *Mary*.

If you are not sure which name to use, then use the surname. Normally the native speaker will suggest you change to first names (*Please, call me Sanne.*). Of course, you can also suggest it, especially if you are older or senior in position.

Note that if you are using surnames, the accepted form for addressing women is *Ms* (pronounced 'Miz'). Always use this form unless a woman says she prefers *Mrs*. *Miss* is hardly ever used now and sounds very old-fashioned.

---

AUDIO

7

**2** **Put the words in the right order to make sentences from the conversation. If necessary, listen again to check your answers.**

1 trouble / us / you / did / any / have / finding / ?

_____

2 website / clear / the / on your / very / were / directions / .

_____

3 your briefcase and coat / leave / my office / can / you / in / .

_____

4 to meet / round / a few members / you / take / team / of the / I'll / .

_____

5 drink / you / to / like / would / something / ?

_____

6 a / of / would / great / coffee / cup / be / .

_____

**3**    Talking about your host's company is a good way to break the ice. Put the words below into the right category.

department • employees • to expand • (ground/first/second) floor • facilities to be founded • lift • location • to move into • neighbourhood • to own • reception • to restructure • staff • stairs

| talking about the building | talking about the company and its history |
|---|---|
| (ground/first/second) floor | department |
| | |
| | |
| | |
| | |
| | |
| | |

Use the correct form of some of the words from the table to complete these mini-dialogues.

Have you been in this _____ [1] long?

No, we actually just _____ [2] this building six months ago. It's a great _____ [3] – lots of green space and some nice cafés nearby.

How many people are in your company now?

How long has your company been around?

It was _____ [4] in 1972.

There are currently around 150 _____ [5]. We have _____ [6] a lot in the last two years.

Which _____ [7] is your office on?

The fifth! Don't worry – we'll take the _____ [8].

Now answer the questions so they are true for you.

AUDIO
8

**4** **Kathrin Oberle, an Austrian lawyer, is visiting a company in London. Complete her parts of the dialogue with sentences (a–g) below. Then listen to check your answers.**

a   Thanks so much for arranging that.
b   And the reception area looks very nice.
c   I managed to get some sleep, actually.
d   Mm. You just don't get tea like this in Austria!
e   Thanks for coming down to meet me.
f   And maybe a glass of water too?
g   Where are you now?

*Carl*   Kathrin, hi. Nice to see you again.

*Kathrin*   Hi, Carl. Nice to see you too.

_____ 1

*Carl*   Always a pleasure! Actually, after the restructuring last year we all got moved around, so I wasn't sure you'd be able to find my office by yourself.

*Kathrin*   Oh, really? _____ 2

*Carl*   On the fourth floor. They decided to put sales and marketing together – at last!

*Kathrin*   That does make more sense, doesn't it? _____

_____ 3

*Carl*   Yes, they finally repainted it in June. … Oh, here's the lift now. After you. Was the driver there to meet you at the airport?

*Kathrin*   Yes, she was. _____ 4

*Carl*   It's the least I could do after your early start! You must be exhausted now.

*Kathrin*   Oh, I'm all right. _____ 5

*Carl*   Here we are … . So, can I get you something to drink? How about a cup of that tea you like so much?

*Kathrin*   That would be wonderful. _____ 6

*Carl*   Coming right up. … Here you are.

*Kathrin*   Oh, thank you.

*Carl*   You're welcome.

*Kathrin*   _____ 7

**Look at the dialogue again. What do you say when …**

a   somebody thanks you? *(three answers)*
b   you want somebody to enter a room or the lift before you?
c   you arrive at your office with your visitor?
d   you give somebody something?
e   somebody gives you something such as food or a drink?

**5**   **Match the questions or comments with the appropriate responses. Sometimes more than one answer is possible.**

1   Did you have any trouble finding us?
2   You can leave your bags at reception.
3   We've been in this building since 1985.
4   I'll take you round later to meet the team.
5   Would you like something to drink?
6   Please help yourself to the biscuits.

a   Mm, thanks. These look delicious.
b   No, thanks. I'm fine.
c   That would be nice, thanks.
d   Great, thank you.
e   No, not at all.
f   Really? How interesting.

**6**   **Now work with a partner to make your own dialogue. Decide whether A and B have met before and use appropriate phrases from the box below.**

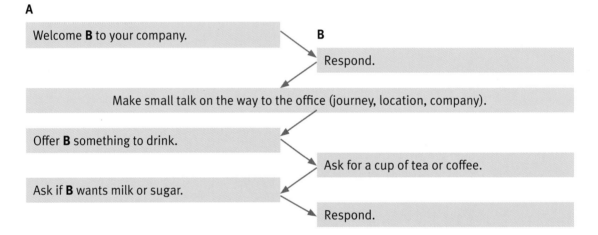

**A**

Welcome **B** to your company.

**B**

Respond.

Make small talk on the way to the office (journey, location, company).

Offer **B** something to drink.

Ask for a cup of tea or coffee.

Ask if **B** wants milk or sugar.

Respond.

---

**WELCOMING VISITORS TO YOUR COMPANY**

**Welcoming a visitor**
Welcome to [*company name*].
Did you have any trouble finding us?
Hello, [*name*]. Nice to see you again.
You can leave your things here/in my office/at the
    reception desk.
I'll take you around to meet the team.

**Offering hospitality**
Would you like something to drink?
How would you like that? Milk/Cream (AmE)?
Sugar?
Here you are.
Please help yourself to the biscuits/cookies (AmE).

**Talking about the offices and company**
It's a lovely space/a very nice location.
The reception area looks very nice.
Have you been in this location long?
How many people work here?
How long has the company been around?

**Accepting hospitality**
A cup of coffee./Some water would be nice.
Just black./With milk and sugar, please.
Thank you./Thanks.

Try to avoid these common mistakes:
~~Welcome in our company.~~           Welcome **to** our company.
~~Are you in this location long?~~     **Have** you **been** in this location long?
~~We are fifty employees.~~            **There** are fifty employees.
~~Please.~~ *(when you give sb sth)*   Here you are.
~~Please.~~ *(when sb thanks you)*     You're welcome./Not at all.

**AUDIO**
9

**7** **Carl is giving Kathrin directions. Listen to the dialogue and complete the sentences.**

1 It's just _____ the corridor, the third door _____ the left.

2 I'll show you _____ it is.

3 But actually, I thought maybe I could just pop _____ Roger's office and say hello.

4 Where is he? – _____ the third floor.

5 So, go _____ the door and turn left to get _____ the lift.

6 Then _____ you come out of the lift, go right, and it's the _____ door on your left.

7 So, I'll meet you _____ here in about ten minutes?

**8** **You are in your office with a visitor. Look at the sketch below and complete the sentences with the correct words.**

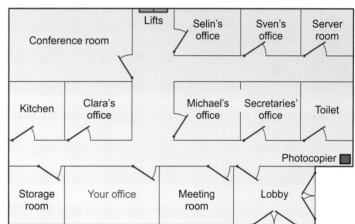

_Clara's office_ ¹?
It's opposite mine.

Go out of the door and
turn left. The _____ ²
is on your right, just past
Clara's office.

Just go out the door
and go straight ahead.
The _____ ³ are at
the end of the corridor.

Go out the
door and turn right.
The _____ ⁴ is
on your left, just after
the lobby.

Turn right when you go out
of my office. The _____ ⁵
is at the end of the corridor
on your right.

**9** **Work with a partner. Use the profiles in the Partner Files to practise giving directions.**

PARTNER FILES    Partner A   File 2, p. 60
                 Partner B   File 2, p. 62

| GIVING DIRECTIONS |
| --- |
| You just go down the corridor and it's right in front of you/on your left/right.<br>It's just down the corridor/round the corner on the left/right.<br>It's the first/second/third door on the left/right.<br>It's next to the toilet/front door/kitchen.<br>Come with me and I'll show you where it is! |

AUDIO

10

**10** **Back in Spain, José María is introducing Sanne to some of his colleagues. Listen and complete the chart below.**

| Name | Title |
|------|-------|
| Valérie | 1 |
| 2 | product designer |
| Greg | 3 |
| 4 | sales manager |

AUDIO

10

**11** **Match the two parts. Then listen again to check.**

1  The first person I'd like you     a  to meet you, Valérie.
2  Valérie, this is     b  assistant, Greg Sánchez.
3  It's a pleasure     c  Sanne Heitink.
4  Have the two of you     d  to get to know everyone better later.
5  It's nice to put     e  quite catch that.
6  Talking of which, this is my     f  to meet is Valérie Dufour.
7  I'm sorry, I didn't     g  a name to a face, isn't it?
8  You'll have a chance     h  met before?

---

**ASKING FOR CLARIFICATION**

When speaking a foreign language, we sometimes need to ask people to repeat things or to explain what they meant by a certain expression or word.

Asking someone to repeat something:
*(I'm) sorry, I didn't quite catch that.*
*(I'm) sorry, could you tell me your name again?*
*Sorry, could you say that for me again?*

You can ask for clarification with these phrases:
*I'm sorry, I don't quite follow you.*
*I'm not totally sure what you mean.*
*If I understand you correctly, you would like us to …*
*Let me see if I've got this right. You would like me to …*

**12**   Complete the mini-dialogues with words from the box.

again • are • catch • could • follow • meant • say • see • sorry • sure

A   My name is Edward Tsipouri.

B   I'm sorry, I didn't quite _____1 that. Tipori, did you _____2?

A   No, Tsipouri. It's a Greek name.

C   Excuse me, Mary. Is there a photocopier nearby?

D   Yes, it's kitty-corner to Jack's office.

C   _____3? I'm not totally _____4 what you mean. Kitty-corner?

D   Oh, it's ... um ... diagonally opposite Jack's office. Here, I'll show you.

E   I'm afraid John's a bit under the weather today.

F   Sorry, I don't quite _____5 you.

E   Oh, sorry. I _____6 that John's ill. He's not coming in today.

F   Oh, I _____7. That's a pity.

G   And I'm Deborah MacGilchrist.

H   I'm sorry, _____8 you tell me your name _____9?

G   MacGilchrist. And you _____10 ...?

H   Barbara, Barbara Kruger. It's very nice to meet you, Ms MacGilchrist.

**13**   Think about the people in your company. Make a list of the colleagues you need to introduce to visitors. Now work with a partner. Take it in turns to introduce the people in your company.

> **INTRODUCTIONS**
>
> **Making introductions**
> I'd like to introduce Sanne Heitink. She's the new head of production.
> The first person I'd like you to meet is [name].
> He's/She's our marketing manager.
> Valérie, this is Sanne Heitink.
> This is Mary, our product designer.
> This is Heather. She'll be your contact person on the IT side of the project.
>
> **Responding to introductions**
> Valérie, this is Sanne Heitink.                    Have the two of you met before?
> – It's a pleasure to meet you, Sanne. (neutral)    – Actually yes, we have.
> – Nice/Good to meet you, Sanne. (informal)         – No, actually we haven't.

**OUTPUT**

**Read the opinions and answer the questions which follow.**

First names are tricky. Everyone's so concerned about intercultural awareness these days that often you have Americans greeting their French counterparts as 'Mr Delatour and 'Ms Lagrange', while the French call the Americans 'Bob' or 'Mary' the first time they meet. But on the other hand, hardly anyone is shocked any more if you don't do what would be normal in 'their' culture.

Visiting companies in the US is always very stressful. People often make little jokes, and I know they're trying to be friendly, but often I don't understand what they mean and then I look like an idiot. I'm sure they think of me as the serious Swiss guy. It's really frustrating.

Coming from Europe, I'm used to being offered a cup of coffee or tea when I visit someone at their company. Perhaps a juice. But I was astonished to arrive at a business colleague's office in Delhi and find a full lunch waiting for me. Have you ever heard of such a thing? I'm not complaining, of course; the food was delicious. Mind you, I don't know what we'll do if the Indian colleague ever visits us!

When you visit someone in a hierarchy-obsessed culture like Japan, it's very easy to tell exactly how important you are to them. Does your counterpart introduce you to her colleagues? OK, not too bad. Does she introduce you to her boss? All right, you can't be that unimportant. And her boss's boss – well, clearly you're someone they're very interested in! But if she doesn't introduce you to anyone, well, that's definitely a bad sign. Japanese people love making introductions!

**OVER TO YOU**

- What problems have you had using first and last names in other cultures?
- What do you offer visitors to eat and drink at your company?
- Do you find it easier to meet native English speakers or non-native English speakers?
- Who would you introduce to your boss? To your boss's boss?

# 3 Getting acquainted

**STARTER** **How well do you know the other people in your group? Ask each other questions and fill in the names of someone who:**

- has a hobby he / she does at least once a week. _____

- enjoys playing a team sport with friends or colleagues. _____

- likes going shopping during the lunch break. _____

- has paintings or photos in his / her office. _____

- never mixes business and pleasure.

  _____

- has become good friends with a business contact. _____

**AUDIO**
**11**

**1** **Sanne Heitink is visiting the Spanish company Salas Design. She and one of the company's product designers, Mary Chan, are in the conference room waiting for a meeting to begin. Listen to their conversation and correct the sentences below.**

1 Anja left the company last June.
2 She lives in Birmingham now.
3 She's working as a programmer for a bicycle manufacturer.
4 Chris is now the marketing manager.
5 He often goes to trade fairs.

**2** Match (1–5) with (a–e) to make questions from the dialogue. Then match them with the answers (A–E).

| 1 Is Anja still | a doing these days? | A She's working as a designer for a bicycle manufacturer. |
| 2 That's near | b doesn't she? | B It's not too far. |
| 3 Do you know | c what she's doing there? | C That's right. |
| 4 How's he | d with the company, by the way? | D He's doing fine. |
| 5 She enjoys sailing, | e you, isn't it? | E She's not, actually. |

AUDIO
11

**3** Here are some more extracts from the dialogue. Complete them with the phrases below. Listen again to check your answers.

> He says hello, by the way.

> I can imagine.

> Not to worry.

> How's he doing these days?

> That's good to hear.

*Mary* Sorry, Sanne, it always takes a few minutes for everyone to arrive.

*Sanne* _____ ¹

*Mary* I heard from her a couple of weeks ago, and she says things are going well.

*Sanne* _____ ² Actually, she did say she wanted to move closer to the sea one day.

*Mary* She took us all out on her boat the weekend before she left. It was a lot of fun.

*Sanne* _____ ³

*Mary* What about Chris? _____ ⁴

*Sanne* He's doing fine. _____ ⁵ He was promoted to product manager recently, so he's in the office more these days.

---

**TALKING ABOUT MUTUAL ACQUAINTANCES**

Talking about mutual acquaintances is a safe small-talk topic, especially with business contacts you do not know very well:

> *How's Marita doing these days?*
> *What's Carol up to?*
> *Have you heard anything from Joe recently?*
> *Say hi to Maria for me. (informal)/Give my regards to Maria. (neutral/formal)*
> *I'm seeing him tomorrow. Should I say hello from you?*

Try to avoid these common mistakes:

| ~~Tell Harry I say hello.~~ | **Say hello/hi to** Harry from me. |
| ~~I haven't seen Claire these last days.~~ | I haven't seen Claire **recently**. |
| ~~How do you do these days?~~ | **How are you doing** these days? |

**4**    **Work with a partner. Use the profiles in the Partner Files to do a role-play. Try to use phrases from the Language Box on page 24.**

**PARTNER FILES** ➤  Partner A    File 3, p. 60
Partner B    File 3, p. 62

MOVING FROM SMALL TALK TO BUSINESS

There is normally a period of small talk at the beginning of a meeting. How long the small talk lasts depends on the culture – it can be as little as five minutes or as long as twenty minutes. At some point, the person who is in charge of the meeting should signal that it's time to start talking about business. Normally there will be a short pause in the conversation, then he/she will say something like:

> *Well, I suppose we should make a start.*
> *So, shall we get down to business?*
> *Right, let's make a start, shall we?*

Note how words like *well*, *so* and *right* are used to show it's time to move on.

**5**    **Talking about what you do in your free time (e.g. hobbies, sport) is a popular topic for small talk. Complete the free-time activities below by writing in the missing vowels (*a, e, i, o, u*). Can you add two more activities to each list?**

| Sport | Relaxing at home | Going out |
|---|---|---|
| sk◻◻ng | l◻st◻n◻ng t◻ m◻s◻c | ◻◻t◻ng ◻◻t |
| d◻◻ng y◻g◻ | r◻◻d◻ng | g◻◻ng t◻ th◻ c◻n◻m◻ |
| k◻◻p◻ng f◻t | w◻tch◻ng t◻l◻v◻s◻◻n | sh◻pp◻ng |
| pl◻y◻ng f◻◻tb◻ll | c◻◻k◻ng | g◻◻ng t◻ c◻nc◻rts |
| _____ | _____ | _____ |
| _____ | _____ | _____ |

**6**    **Complete the sentences with the correct form of *do*, *go*, or *play*.**

1   Are there any nice places to _____ running around here?

2   My daughter and I enjoy _____ chess.

3   _____ you ever _____ tai chi? I really enjoy it.

4   How often _____ you _____ to the gym?

5   I _____ the piano since I was a child.

6   Last summer we _____ windsurfing almost every day.

7   I used to _____ aerobics when I was younger.

8   I wish I had time to _____ more sport.

---

**FREE-TIME ACTIVITIES**

**Asking about free-time activities**
So, what do you like doing in your free time?
Do you have any hobbies?
Do you do any sports?
What do you do to keep fit?

**Talking about free-time activities**
I love/(don't) like/hate cooking/watching TV.
I often go to the gym/do yoga after work/at the weekend.
I like going to the theatre but I hardly ever have the time.
I try to play football/squash at least once a week.

Try to avoid these common mistakes:

| | |
|---|---|
| ~~I like looking television.~~ | I like **watching** television. |
| ~~I hate making fitness.~~ | I hate **going to the gym**. |
| ~~I often go in the cinema.~~ | I often go **to** the cinema. |
| ~~I like it to read books in English.~~ | I like **reading** books in English. |

---

**7** Work with a partner to make a dialogue. A and B are waiting for a meeting to begin and are chatting until the other participants arrive. (A is in charge of the meeting.)

**A**

| Greet **B** and ask how he/she is. |
|---|

**B**

| Respond. Ask **A** how he/she is. |
|---|

| Respond. Ask about **B**'s journey. |
|---|

| Respond. Say something about the weather. |
|---|

| Respond. Ask about your partner's hobbies. |
|---|

| Respond. Ask about a mutual acquaintance/ a colleague you both know. |
|---|

| Respond. (The other participants have arrived.) Say it's time to begin. |
|---|

| Agree. |
|---|

AUDIO
12–14

**8** **The meeting participants are having a break. Listen to the dialogues. Who:**

- offers Sanne a coffee?

  _____ 1

- needs to go to the toilet?

  _____ 2

- has a friend who is an artist?

  _____ 3

- wants to buy a birthday present?

  _____ 4

- likes jazz?

  _____ 5

- went to Amsterdam on a school trip?

  _____ 6

**9** **Complete these sentences from the dialogues. Listen again if necessary.**

1  _____ start again at, _____ , 3.30?

2  _____ you a coffee, Sanne?

3  That _____ , thanks Mary.

4  _____ your toilet?

5  _____ your coffee. _____ black, right?

6  That's an interesting painting you've _____ , José María.

7  I can give you his phone number _____ .

8  Is this your _____ in Spain?

9  Was that for business _____ ?

10  Have you _____ to the Netherlands?

---

**ADMIRING PERSONAL POSSESSIONS**

In Britain and the USA it is acceptable to compliment your host on personal objects in his/her home or office, and this is a common small-talk topic when visiting someone. However, in some cultures (e.g. the Middle East or Thailand), it is better not to admire a personal object openly. If you do, the host may feel obliged to give it to you.

**10**   Talking about places you have visited is a common small-talk topic. Choose one line from each column to make mini-dialogues.

| Person A | Person B | Person A |
|---|---|---|
| 1  So is this your first time in Switzerland? | a  Yes, very much. Especially the food! | A  I know. It's terrible, isn't it? |
| 2  Have you ever been to Canada? | b  No, this is my first time. What about you? | B  That's good. At least you had some time to relax. |
| 3  Did you enjoy your visit to Munich? | c  No, it was actually a business trip. But I had a couple of days free. | C  Oh really? Was that for business or pleasure? |
| 4  Have you been here before? | d  We found this fantastic hotel right next to the river. | D  It's my first time here as well. |
| 5  What did you think of Edinburgh? | e  Actually, I was here once before, in 2001. | E  Sounds great! Do you remember the name? |
| 6  Were you there on holiday? | f  It's an amazing city. Pity about the weather though! | F  You should. It's really a great country. |
| 7  Where did you stay when you were there? | g  No, but I'd love to go there sometime. | G  I know, it's delicious, isn't it? |

---

**KEEPING THE CONVERSATION GOING**

Here are some ways to keep the conversation going.
- When someone asks you a question, ask them the question back as well:
  *Have you ever been to Hong Kong?*
  *No, I haven't.* ***What about you?***

- Give some extra information when you answer the question:
  *I was there in '98.* ***I stayed in this great place in the old town.***

- Use question tags to encourage the other person to speak:
  *The food in France is great,* ***isn't it?***
  *I know. I ate so much when I was there!*

---

**11**   Look at the questions and think of responses that will keep the conversation going.

1  So, have you ever been to Italy?

2  Do you enjoy going to the theatre?

3  Is this weather typical for the time of year?

4  Do you play tennis?

**12** The sentences below are taken from the emails José María and Sanne wrote to thank each other for the visit. Decide who wrote each sentence, José María (J) or Sanne (S).

[S] a  I hope that I will be able to return the favour

[ ] b  I hope you had a good trip back to Holland

[ ] c  I just wanted to say thank you for inviting me to your company last week

[ ] d  I really enjoyed having you visit the company

[ ] e  I enjoyed the chance to meet your team

[ ] f  Please give my best to Mary, Valérie, Emin and Greg

**Now complete the emails using the sentences above.**

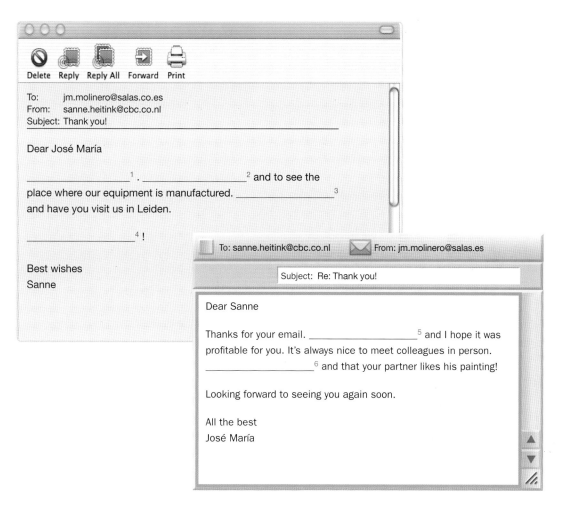

To:      jm.molinero@salas.co.es
From:    sanne.heitink@cbc.co.nl
Subject: Thank you!

Dear José María

_____ 1 . _____ 2 and to see the
place where our equipment is manufactured. _____ 3
and have you visit us in Leiden.

_____ 4 !

Best wishes
Sanne

To: sanne.heitink@cbc.co.nl     From: jm.molinero@salas.es

Subject:  Re: Thank you!

Dear Sanne

Thanks for your email. _____ 5 and I hope it was
profitable for you. It's always nice to meet colleagues in person.
_____ 6 and that your partner likes his painting!

Looking forward to seeing you again soon.

All the best
José María

**13** Think of a business contact you know. Imagine you have been to visit him/her at his/her company. Write a thank-you email. Use the emails from exercise 12 as models.

**Read the article and discuss the questions which follow.**

# Small talk made simple

*In theory, making small talk in English isn't rocket science. All you need to do is say hello and ask a few questions: 'Where are you from?' 'Do you like it there?' 'How did you get into engineering/marketing/metallurgy?'*

*Of course, in practice it can be more difficult. Maybe the person you're trying to speak to keeps replying with one-word answers. Maybe you always seem to meet people in noisy conference halls where you can hardly hear what they're saying, let alone understand it. Or maybe – and this seems to happen to a lot of people – you can talk about your job for hours, but feel much less secure making chit-chat.*

*What can you do to solve these problems? Well, there are a lot of things you can try.*

*Is this your first time here?*

*What a wonderful event!*

*Please, call me Pedro.*

### Watch the pros ...
Observe people who are confident speaking English. How do they talk? Contribute, of course, but listen, and note the questions they ask. Also think about their intonation – the way they use their voice to convey meaning. Is it something you can try yourself?

### ... and the stars
Of course, your colleagues from London will think you're crazy if you start writing down things they say. ' "Please, call me Bill," did you say? Oh that's quite good ...' But actors don't mind this at all. So the next time you're in the video shop, try borrowing an English-language DVD. Watch it with subtitles, and pay attention to the way people interact.

### Listen and learn
While you're at it, do more than watch: repeat what you hear the actors say. Then record yourself and play it back. (Most laptops and MP3 players have built-in microphones.) It might be a bit embarrassing at first, but this is the best way to become aware of your speech and how it sounds to others. Compare your pronunciation to the one on the CD or DVD, and try again. You'll be impressed at how quickly you improve.

### Practice makes perfect
Easier said than done, but really: don't be shy. The more you say during the coffee break, the more confident you'll feel about making conversation at lunch. ∎

**OVER TO YOU**

- What tips can you add?
- What ideas have you tried to make socializing in English easier? What has worked for you?
- Do you know anyone who is good at socializing in English? What makes them so effective?

# 4 Entertaining a visitor

STARTER

**Answer the questions about entertaining a visitor. Then ask a partner.**

|  | me | my partner |
|---|---|---|
| 1 Who were the last business visitors you had? |  |  |
| 2 How did you socialize with them? (go for dinner, see a concert, etc.) |  |  |
| 3 What did you talk about? |  |  |
| 4 What did you *not* talk about? (family, politics, work, etc.) |  |  |
| 5 Was it easy or difficult to look after the visitors? Why? |  |  |

AUDIO
15–17

**1** **Rolf and Jessica are showing their American visitor, Phillip, around their town. Listen to the dialogues and match them to places on the map.**

Conversation 1 ☐

Conversation 2 ☐

Conversation 3 ☐

**Read the extracts from the tourist brochure. Rolf and Jessica made three mistakes in the information they told Phillip. What were they? Listen again if necessary.**

A **Schwarzburg Arkaden (shopping centre)**
- Built in 2002
- More than 20 shops and restaurants

B **Schloss Schwarzburg (Schwarzburg castle)**
- Built by King Heinrich the First in 1743
- Partially destroyed during World War Two
- Rebuilt in the 1960s

C **Schwarzburg Art Gallery**
- Designed by the American architect Renzo Kindeslieb
- Building was a brewery (closed in 1994)

D **Rathaus (Town Hall)**
- Built in 1834
- Often has exhibitions open to the public

E **Schwarzburg Cathedral**
- Built between 1510 and 1543
- Services on Sundays at 8 a.m. and 10 a.m.

AUDIO
15–17

**2**   **Complete the sentences from the dialogues in exercise 1 with the words below. There are some words you do not need. Listen to the dialogues again if necessary.**

actually • building • built • designed • destroyed • shut • supposed • telling • that • this • typical

1   _____ is the cathedral here.

2   This kind of architecture is _____ of our region.

3   That's the castle I was _____ you about earlier.

4   It was _____ by King Heinrich the Second.

5   It was almost completely _____ by bombing in the war.

6   Part of the _____ used to be a brewery.

7   The brewery _____ in 1992 after reunification.

8   The building is _____ to look like a beer bottle.

**3**   **Think of five interesting places in your town or city. Prepare a short talk providing details about them such as key dates, historical facts, and interesting data. Use the Internet if you need to check your information. Present your information to the rest of the class and give them a 'virtual' tour of your town.**

**USED TO**

We use the phrase *used to* when we are talking about things which were true in the past but are not true now. We use it a lot when socializing, especially when talking about our lives or the history of our town:

> *I used to live in Amsterdam.*
> *Part of the building used to be a brewery.*
> *Steel used to be a big industry here in Sheffield.*

**4** **Talking about the place where you live or work is a popular small-talk topic. Use the following words and phrases to complete the sentences below. You can use some words more than once.**

airport      close to      about the same size as      conference centre

regional      small      much smaller than      on      near

harbour      beautiful      university      state      a bit bigger than

castle

industrial      large      important      cathedral      national      historic

My town/city has a(n) _____

_____

_____

_____

_____

_____

It's a(n) _____ town/city.

_____

_____

_____

_____

It's _____ Oxford/London.

_____

_____

_____

It's the _____ capital.

_____

_____

It's _____ the Danube/Rhine.

_____

It's _____ the Czech Republic/France.

_____

_____

**Can you add more words to any of the lists? Now write a short text about your town or city.**

---

**USING TOURIST INFORMATION**

Many cities have tourist information brochures available in English. Visit your local tourist office or their website to see what they have. Or, if your town or city is popular with tourists, visit travel websites such as *www.lonelyplanet.com* or *www.roughguides.com* to see what they say about where you live. It's a good way to learn the vocabulary you need to tell visitors about your town.

---

**5**  Imagine you are showing your partner around the place where you live or work. Tell him/her about three sights in your town/city. If you like, draw a simple map to use as a reference.

---

**SHOWING VISITORS AROUND**

If we go along here, we come to …
On your left/right you can see …
The [*place*] is right in front of you/on your left/right.
The [*building*] is opposite the …
The castle/church/… was built by … in …
… is famous for …
The …  is open to visitors from … to …

Try to avoid these common mistakes:

| | |
|---|---|
| ~~The town hall is on your right side.~~ | The town hall is on your **right**. |
| ~~The museum is opposite from the cathedral.~~ | The museum is **opposite** the cathedral. |
| ~~The theatre was designed from a Danish architect.~~ | The theatre was designed **by** a Danish architect. |

---

AUDIO
18

**6**  Two Italians are showing Sharon, an American visitor, around their town. Listen and decide if the statements are true or false. Correct the false statements.

1  Both Mauro and Cristina are from Modena.

2  Cristina went to university in Milano.

3  Cristina finds Modena a bit small.

4  Sharon agrees to go to a museum with Mauro.

5  Sharon decides to go to an art exhibition.

**AUDIO**
**18**

## 7 Match the two parts to make sentences from the dialogue. Listen again if necessary.

| | | | |
|---|---|---|---|
| 1 | So are you both | a | like living here? |
| 2 | How long | b | university in Torino. |
| 3 | I went to | c | from Modena originally? |
| 4 | When I graduated | d | it exactly? |
| 5 | And do you | e | I moved to Modena. |
| 6 | That's something | f | on a farm. |
| 7 | I grew up | g | have you lived here? |
| 8 | Where is | h | I miss in a city. |

## 8 Work with a partner. Ask your partner some or all of the following questions to find out about their life. Make a note of the answers.

Are you from [*name of town/city*] originally?
How long have you lived here?
Where did you live before that?
Did you go to college/university/vocational
    school in [*name of town/city*]?
What did you study?
Do you like living here?
Do you ever miss [*name of place*]?
What do you do in your free time?

I grew up in …

I graduated from [*institution*] in [*year*].

I was born in …

I went to university in …

I live in/near/not far from …

**Now tell the class about your partner, but include three things which are not true.**
**Can the others guess what they are?**

For example:
A   So Suzanne was born in Paris.
B   That's not true. I think she was born in Brussels.
A   You're right! She was born in Brussels and moved to Paris when she was ten.

---

**TALKING ABOUT ORIGINS**

Talking about people's origins can be a very complicated and sensitive area. Here are some tips:

- It is very impolite (and offensive) to ask non-white British or American people where they are 'really' from, or to guess where their family is from.
- Americans of African descent generally refer to themselves as *African-American* (but not ~~Afro-American~~) or 'black'. The words *coloured* and *Negro* are no longer used and are considered offensive by most people.
- British people of African or Caribbean descent generally refer to themselves as *Black British*.
- Remember that the UK is England, Scotland, Wales, and Northern Ireland. So a *British* person can be from any of these countries, and (for example) a *Scottish* person is also 'British' but not English. Never ask a Scottish person 'Which part of England are you from?'!

**AUDIO**
18

**9** In the dialogue in exercise 6, Mauro and Cristina also tell Sharon about some things she can do in Modena. Complete the sentences from the dialogue with the words below. Listen again if necessary.

> country • fair • free • love • museum • nice • pick • really •
> recommendations • say • sounds • take

1 If we have time, perhaps we can drive out into the _____.

2 That would be _____ .

3 I've actually got the afternoon _____ tomorrow.

4 I was wondering if you had any _____ for things to do.

5 There's a fantastic car _____ at Panzano, which is not far from here.

6 I can _____ you if you like.

7 The antique _____ is on tomorrow.

8 It's _____ good.

9 That _____ great. I _____ antiques.

10 I'll _____ you up at the hotel. _____ ten?

**Which sentences are said by ...**

• the host?   _1,_____

• the guest?   _2,_____

**10** Work with a partner to practise making recommendations. Try to use phrases from the Language Box on the next page.

*Partner A:* Write down three things visitors can do in the town or city where you work or live. Tell your partner what they are and why they are interesting. If your partner wants to see one of the things, then give them directions how to get there.

*Partner B:* Show interest in what your partner is saying.

**Now change roles.**

---

**RECOMMENDATIONS**

**Recommending places to see**
There's a(n) great/fantastic/interesting
    exhibition/art gallery/museum/
    restaurant/café/shop/park/street.
It's really worth visiting/seeing/a visit.

**Reacting to recommendations**
That sounds (really) nice/great/interesting.
I'll definitely do that.
I'll definitely go there.
I'd love to see that.

**Giving directions**
It's next to/near/close to/just around the corner from the town hall/square.
It's on the same street as your hotel/the station.
Just go along this street/the High Street, then turn left/right.

Try to avoid these common mistakes:
~~It gives a fantastic exhibition at the castle.~~    **There's** a fantastic exhibition at the castle.
~~It's really worth to visit.~~    It's really worth **visiting**.
~~It is in the near of the town hall.~~    It's **near** the town hall.

---

AUDIO
19–22

**11**  **Hosts often invite their guests to join them in social activities. Listen to four invitations and complete the chart.**

|  | Conversation 1 | Conversation 2 | Conversation 3 | Conversation 4 |
|---|---|---|---|---|
| a  What invitation does the host make? |  |  |  |  |
| b  Does the guest accept or turn down the invitation? |  |  |  |  |
| c  What excuse does the guest give (if any)? |  |  |  |  |
| d  What alternative does the guest suggest (if any)? |  |  |  |  |

**Now order the sentences from the conversations. If necessary, listen again to check your answers.**

1   for dinner / if / to join / would like / tonight / us / I was / wondering / you / .

2   meeting / week / How about / a coffee / next / for / ?

3   an / for / have / I / opera / extra / the / ticket / tonight / .

4   come / like / you / to / Would / ?

5   and I / Saturday / are / My / next / partner / a party / having / .

6   come / could / hoping / were / We / you / .

### INVITATIONS

**Accepting invitations**

*That would be lovely.*

*Thank you, I'd like that very much.*

*That sounds great, thanks.*

*Good idea. Let's do that.*

**Turning down invitations**

It is more difficult to say 'no' to invitations and still be polite.

Here are some examples of how to turn down an invitation:

| 1 thank the person | | 2 give a reason | 3 offer an alternative |
|---|---|---|---|
| *That's really kind of you* | *but* | *my flight's at 6 p.m. so I should probably stay in town just to make sure I get to the airport in time.* | *Perhaps we can do it next time I'm in town.* |
| *That's very nice of you* | *but actually* | *I'm afraid my boss wants my report first thing tomorrow so I need to stay at the hotel and write that.* | *But maybe we could go for dinner tomorrow instead?* |
| *I'd love to (come)* | *however* | *I'm afraid I just don't have time today.* | *How about having lunch sometime next week?* |

**12** **Rewrite B's responses to make them more polite.**

1  A  So, shall we have dinner together tonight?

   B  ~~I can't. I have to get up early tomorrow.~~

   *That would be really nice, but I'm afraid I have a meeting first thing tomorrow and I have to go to bed early.*

2  A  How about some lunch?

   B  ~~No, I don't have time.~~

3  A  I'm having friends over for a barbecue this evening. Would you like to come?

   B  ~~No, I have to prepare a presentation.~~

4  A  We're going for a drink. Would you like to join us?

   B  ~~Impossible. I'm meeting someone else.~~

**13** **Work with a partner. Use the profiles in the Partner Files to do a role-play. Try to use phrases from this unit to make and turn down or accept invitations.**

**PARTNER FILES** Partner A   File 4, p. 61
Partner B   File 4, p. 63

OUTPUT

**Read this article from an American magazine and discuss the questions which follow.**

# Making business personal

**Business is always personal, and opening up to your business contacts is the best way to develop your business relationships. Kelly Watson argues why you should stop trying to keep your business life and your family life separate.**

'Dienst ist Dienst und Schnaps ist Schnaps' is a famous German saying. Work is work, and socializing is socializing, and the two worlds should never meet, right? Wrong! Treating business contacts differently from personal friends is one of the most common mistakes business people make. Think about your business contacts who are also friends of yours. Isn't it easier to do business with them? Don't they help you and tolerate your mistakes more than casual acquaintances? Exactly! So make your business relationships more personal and you will find your work is easier and that you are more successful.

But how can you make business more personal? Easy! Do the same things you would do when making 'real' friends. Show that you're human, not just a face in a suit. Create intimacy between you and the business contact and you will create trust. Instead of just making superficial small talk, talk about the things which are really important to you: your family, your hobbies, your problems, and worries.

And don't be afraid to introduce your business contacts to your friends and family. John Zimmerman, who is CEO of a technology company in Seattle and a good friend of mine, began taking his daughter, Laura, on business trips with him so that they could spend more time together. Dinner conversations became more personal because his business contacts wanted to talk to Laura. John's contacts told him about their families, and one manager's son even became Laura's pen friend.

Everyone was a winner with this scenario. Not only did John spend more time with his daughter, but she learned a lot about his work and the world of business. And John's business contacts now invite John and his daughter to spend time with their families, taking those business relationships to another level.

So don't be afraid to mix your business life with your personal life. OK, so you might not be able to give a sales presentation over dinner if your friends or family

are there. But it doesn't matter: when it comes to business, it's the personal relationship that makes all the difference. Mixing your business life with your personal life benefits everybody: you, your business contacts and your family. ■

OVER TO YOU

- Do you ever mix your business and personal lives? How many of your business contacts have met your family or friends?
- Would you ever take a member of your family with you on a business trip?
- Is it easier to do business with friends than casual acquaintances? What are the advantages and disadvantages?
- How can business people balance work commitments with private/family life?

# 5 Eating out

**Which of the places below would you take the following guests to for dinner? Discuss with a partner.**

- a group of British engineers
- an important Indian customer
- colleagues from your American subsidiary
- an international group of young people doing work experience at your company
- a group of high-ranking government officials from Lithuania

---

### Finnegan's Wake

 Enjoy the 'craic' at our fun Irish pub!

•

Large screen TV showing all big sporting events.

•

Happy hour 7–8 p.m. every day.
Two pints of Guinness for the price of one.

---

### Zweighof

**Traditional German, Swiss and Austrian specialities**

—

20 different beers on tap

Large groups catered for

---

### The Bleeding Heart

The best steak in town – cooked at your table. Special meat buffet on Wednesday nights. Free side dish with every steak.

---

### FORAGE

Sophisticated modern vegetarian and vegan cuisine in an elegant setting.

All dishes prepared with organic local produce.

Innovative salad and juice bars.

---

### Lee's 'Krazy Karaoke Kavern'

- Fun karaoke bar with over 20,000 songs to choose from!
- Friday night is fancy dress karaoke night - everyone who comes in fancy dress gets a free pitcher of beer!
- Office parties welcome!

---

### Phitsanulok

FINE, AUTHENTIC, FULL-FLAVOURED THAI CUISINE.

We use the very best ingredients with fresh herbs, spices and vegetables sent directly to us from growers in Thailand.

---

### L'Aurore

Michelin-starred restaurant with award-winning interior.

Seasonal dishes created by star chef André Rogal.

Extensive wine list to complement our meals.    Reservations required

---

**Now think of your own foreign business contacts. Where would you take them? Why?**

AUDIO

23

**1**  **Bruno and Carlo are entertaining Anna at a local restaurant. Listen to the conversation and answer the questions below.**

1  Have the hosts been to the restaurant before?
2  Why is Anna hungry?
3  What do we discover about Bruno's wife?
4  Who is driving?
5  What do they plan to do later?

**Complete this table with their orders.**

|  | Starter | Main course | Drink |
|---|---|---|---|
| **Anna** |  |  |  |
| **Bruno** |  |  |  |
| **Carlo** |  |  |  |

**2**  **Match the two halves to make sentences from the dialogue. Listen again if necessary.**

1  This looks
2  I hope
3  I'm absolutely
4  I'm afraid they don't have
5  How many courses
6  What do you
7  It comes with asparagus
8  I'll have the soup
9  What would you like
10  Let's see if we can

a  are we having, Carlo?
b  to drink?
c  followed by the pasta.
d  recommend?
e  catch the waiter's attention.
f  menus in English here.
g  you like it.
h  starving.
i  a really nice place.
j  and small potatoes roasted in the oven.

**3** Look at the descriptions of different dishes below. Can you guess what each dish is?

**1** So this is a Swiss speciality. You get a pot with melted cheese and then you dip pieces of bread into the cheese and eat them. It's great at parties or when you have a group of people.

**2** This is a typical Italian dish. It's made with flat sheets of pasta with tomato sauce in between. It also has a white sauce and maybe some cheese on top.

**3** This is an Indian speciality popular in the West, especially in the UK. You have meat or vegetables in a spicy sauce. Often the sauce is made with cream. It's served with rice.

Think of three dishes and explain them to your partner. Can they guess what they are?

| EXPLAINING A MENU | |
| --- | --- |
| This is a local speciality. | It's made with meat/fish/vegetables. |
| It's typical of/a speciality of our region. | It's a bit like spaghetti/pudding/rice/pizza. |
| It's a spicy/savoury/sweet dish. | It's a light/dark/wheat beer. |
| It's a kind of pasta/meat/dumpling. | It's juice mixed with mineral water. |

**4** Sort the words into the correct categories in the table below.

bake    sweet    rich    rice

~~beef~~    potato wedges    roast    pork

pepper    grill (BrE)/broil (AmE)    starter (BrE)/appetizer (AmE)    onion

cabbage    courgette (BrE)/zucchini (AmE)    salad    main course

chicken    chips (BrE)/French fries (AmE)    savoury    light

~~dessert~~    fry    ham    spicy    lamb

| parts of the meal | types of meat | types of vegetable | side dishes | ways of cooking | words for describing food |
| --- | --- | --- | --- | --- | --- |
| dessert | beef | | | | |
| | | | | | |
| | | | | | |
| | | | | | |

Can you add more words to the categories in the table?

**5**   **Work with a partner to role-play the start of a business lunch. Explain the menu to your partner and decide what you will order.**

---

**AT A RESTAURANT**

| **Helping with the menu** | **Deciding what to order** |
|---|---|
| Let me know if you need any help with the menu. | Do you know what you're having? |
| Oh, that. It's a kind of fish. | Have you decided yet? |
| It's (a bit) like an omelette. | That's what I'm going to have for my starter. |
| Do you know ravioli? Well, it's similar to that. | I think I'll have that for the main course. |
| It's made with eggs, milk and sugar. | I'm going to have the dish of the day (BrE)/special (AmE) |

Try to avoid these common mistakes:

| ~~Waiter!~~ | **Excuse me.** |
|---|---|
| ~~Give us the menu.~~ | Can we **have/see** the menu, please? |
| ~~I don't eat pig.~~ | I don't eat **pork**. |
| ~~I take the pasta.~~ | **I'll have** the pasta. |
| ~~I'd like water with/without gas.~~ | I'd like **sparkling/still** water. |

---

AUDIO
24

**6**   **Anna, Bruno and Carlo are finishing their meal. Tick ✔ the topics they talk about.**

the restaurant ☐          friends ☐

holidays ☐          sport ☐

family ☐          cultural differences ☐

mutual acquaintances ☐          their jobs ☐

**Now complete the sentences from the dialogue. Listen again if necessary.**

1   So, how _____ the tuna?

2   Oh, it was very _____ and _____ cooked.

3   So do _____ often?

4   What _____ , Bruno?

5   So _____ well, Carlo?

6   You _____ earlier.

7   Really?  We _____ for our holiday.

8   Do _____ Anna?

9   You _____ to Croatia last year.

10   _____ France, I've still got room for _____ .

**7** Talking about your family is a good small-talk subject and helps to develop a relationship. How much 'family vocabulary' do you know? Work with a partner to do this quiz.

## Look at the words below.

> acquaintance ▪ divorced ▪ married ▪ mother-in-law ▪ only child ▪ relations ▪ relatives ▪ separated ▪ single ▪ step-son

Can you find:

**1** four words for types of marital status?

_____  _____

_____  _____

**2** two other words for 'family members'?

_____  _____

**3** words that match these definitions?
**a** someone who you know but is not a friend

_____

**b** the mother of your husband or wife

_____

**c** a girl or boy who has no brothers or sisters

_____

**d** a son your husband or wife has from a previous marriage _____

## Now complete the sentences.

**4** My partner _____ a baby next year.

**5** My wife's brother, in other words my _____ , lives in Australia.

**6** After the meeting, some of the guys are meeting their _____ for dinner. Mine had to stay at home with the children, so I'll just get room service.

**7** My son's going out with his first _____ .

**8** I feel sorry for _____ . It's easier with brothers or sisters.

**8** Work with a partner. Draw part of your family tree with at least five people (or write down the names of five people in your family). Then take it in turns to ask each other questions about your families.

> I have two daughters. Let me show you a picture.

| TALKING ABOUT FAMILY | |
|---|---|
| Do you have any brothers or sisters? | [name] got married in [year]. |
| Is [name] married? | He/She has ... children. |
| Does [name] have any children? | He/She is single. |
| How old is [name]? | They are married/living together/separated/divorced. |
| Where does [name] live? | He/She is ... years old. |

---

**KEEPING A CONVERSATION GOING**

Sometimes it can be difficult to keep a conversation going, especially if your conversation partner is not very good at socializing. Here are some tips for avoiding awkward silences.

- When someone asks you a question, usually it is because they are genuinely interested so don't just give a simple answer. Give some extra information and/or ask another question in return:

  A  *How long have you been working here?*
  B  *About three years. Before that I was actually working for the competition. What about you? How long have you been with your company?*

- If someone offers 'extra' information when answering your question, ask another follow-up question:

  A  *This is a great restaurant. Do you come here often?*
  B  *Oh yes. I was here last week actually.*
  A  *Oh really? Was that for business or pleasure?*

- If the conversation 'dies', you can start a new topic by referring to or asking about something that was said earlier:

  *So, are you married, Marco? You mentioned your mother-in-law earlier.*
  *You were saying earlier that you spent some time in Africa.*

**9**  **The answers to the questions below are too short. Make them longer by adding extra information and a question, as in the example.**

1  A  So, do you live near here?
   B  Yes, I do.
      [*only 2 km*]  *Our house is only two kilometres from here.*
      [*you/live?*]  *What about you? Do you live near your work?*

2  A  And how old is your daughter?
   B  She's six.
      [*recently started school*]
      [*you/children?*]

3  A  What kind of dog do you have?
   B  An Alsatian.
      [*fun but needs lots of exercise*]
      [*you/pets?*]

4  A  So, how long have you been with the company?
   B  Six years.
      [*joined after university*]
      [*you/be with your company long?*]

5  A  Have you ever been to Moscow?
   B  Yes, I have.
      [*three years ago/on business*]
      [*you?*]

6  A  And do you do any sports?
   B  I play squash
      [*once a week with friends*]
      [*you/sports?*]

7  A  It's so hot today. Is it normally like this in the summer here?
   B  No, it's not.
      [*very hot for us/usually 25 degrees*]
      [*weather/where you live?*]

**10**  Commenting on what people say is a good way to keep a conversation going.
Match B's comments to what A says. Sometimes more than one answer is possible.

**A**

1   I just got married last year actually.
2   My husband is a meteorologist.
3   Last year I won a prize for one of the products I designed.
4   The project deadline is next week and we're not going to make it.
5   My daughter has just got a place at one of the best universities in the country.
6   Before I got this job I was unemployed for two years.
7   I went to Peru on holiday last year.

**B**

a   That must be very stressful.
b   Really? That's an interesting job!
c   Oh, congratulations!
d   You must be very proud of her.
e   That must have been very exciting.
f   You must have felt very pleased.
g   Oh, I'm sorry to hear that. I imagine that was a difficult time for you.

When do we say *that must be …* and when *that must have been …*?

**11**  Work with a partner to make small talk at a restaurant. Use the information in the Partner Files to ask questions and keep the conversation going.

**PARTNER FILES**   Partner A   File 5, p. 61
Partner B   File 5, p. 63

AUDIO
25

**12**  Anna, Bruno and Carlo are ready to pay. Listen and decide if the statements below are true or false.

1   Both Anna and Bruno are tired.
2   They all want a coffee.
3   Anna wants to pay.
4   She doesn't want to leave a tip.
5   In the end, Anna doesn't pay.

**13** Complete the sentences from the dialogue with the correct form of verbs from the box. You will need to use some verbs more than once.

be • catch • get • have • put • round

1 I'll _____ one with the bill.

2 Let me try and _____ the waiter.

3 Let me _____ this.

4 Seriously, it _____ on me.

5 You _____ very welcome.

6 I'm going to _____ it on expenses any way.

7 Just _____ up the total.

8 But I don't _____ any cash on me!

---

**BUT SERIOUSLY ...**

We say *seriously* when we want to emphasize that we really mean something (for example when we are trying to persuade someone to accept an offer):

> *Seriously, this is on me.*
> *Seriously, I can take you to the airport. It's no problem.*

We can also say it after a joke:

> *That's a brilliant suggestion – I'm going to tell everyone I thought of it. But seriously, I do think it's a good idea.*
> *Our lorries are so slow the food is out of date before it arrives. But seriously, we do have problems with delivery times.*

Note that in many cultures humour is very important in socializing. But, different cultures tend to have very different senses of humour, and jokes often don't 'translate' well from one culture to another. As an example, the British like self-deprecating humour where a person makes jokes about him or herself. The British can also be very sarcastic in social situations and make fun of each other – to the outsider this can seem rather aggressive.

---

**14** You are in a restaurant in the UK with a business contact and it's time to pay. Work with a partner to make a dialogue.

**AT THE END OF A MEAL**

**Asking for the bill**
Can we have the bill, please?
Could you bring us the bill, please (when you have a moment)?

**Offering to pay**
Let me/I'll get this.
This is on me.

**Thanking someone for a meal**
That was lovely, thank you.
That's very nice of you to pay.

**Responding to thanks**
You're (very) welcome.
It was a pleasure.

Try to avoid these common mistakes:

| | |
|---|---|
| I invite you. | I'll get this./This is on me./It's my treat. |
| Please. | You're welcome. *(when responding to thanks)* |
| The food tasted very well. | The food was very good/great/fantastic. |

**OUTPUT**   **Look at what these people are saying about socializing in restaurants. Which opinion(s) do you agree with?**

I hate it when I'm having dinner in a restaurant with business contacts and it's time to pay. It's never completely clear who's going to get the bill. You have to offer to pay, but then the others have to say that they'll pay. Often I can't tell if they mean it or not, and I don't know if I should pay or let them pay. It's really embarrassing.

Eating with business contacts from another country is very stressful, in my opinion. It's such a cultural thing, and there are a hundred little rules you have to follow, otherwise people think you're impolite. I'm always so worried that I never enjoy my meal!

I love eating out with business contacts. It's always a real chance to get to know them as people. I like the fact that you can talk about things other than business. And it's interesting to learn about the food in their country – that's always a good topic of conversation.

Sometimes I find it difficult to know how much to tip when I'm in a foreign country. It's especially difficult when you're not sure how much the money is worth. But normally I ask the people I'm with and they give me some advice.

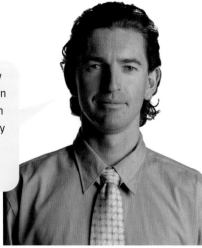

**OVER TO YOU**

- What other eating and dining habits have you noticed in other countries?
- Who pays when you go to dinner with business contacts?
- How much do you normally tip in restaurants in your country? What about in other countries you've visited?

#  6 Networking at a trade fair

**Look at the networking tips below. Do you agree/disagree with them? Which are the best tips?**

## Steps to successful networking

**1** Prepare a 30-second 'verbal business card': *'Hi, I'm Shara Lacey. I'm the CTO of GreenFire Systems. We provide …'.*

**2** Offer your name when you introduce yourself. You know who you are, but other people don't!

**3** Are you feeling shy and lonely? Look for someone who is alone, and speak to them.

**4** Focus on other people rather than yourself. Listen to what they're saying instead of thinking about what you want to say next.

**5** Ask questions. You learn more by listening than by talking.

**6** Wear comfortable clothes. You won't make a good impression if you don't feel good in what you are wearing.

**7** Remember to give people your business card. But ask for their card first.

**8** Make eye contact.

**9** Smile!

**10** Practise! The more networking you do, the better you will be!

**1** Here are some topics you can use to begin a conversation at a trade fair. Can you think of any others?

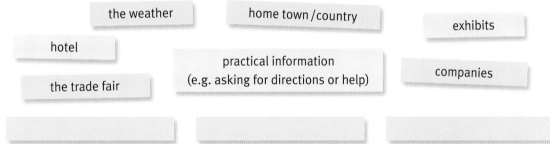

the weather

home town / country

exhibits

hotel

practical information
(e.g. asking for directions or help)

companies

the trade fair

Now match these statements used to begin a conversation with the topics above.
Think of statements for the other topics.

1 I noticed that your name tag says you work for Jansch Networks.
2 Excuse me, do you know how to operate this ticket machine?
3 What a beautiful day! It's too bad we're stuck in here.
4 Are you staying at the Four Seasons as well?
5 This looks very interesting. What is it exactly?
6 Are you here for the electronics show?
7 Excuse me, are you American? I heard you speaking English …

AUDIO

26–28

**2** Ute Adena is the head of purchasing for a large electronics firm in Germany. Listen to three conversations she has at a trade fair in Milan. Which of the topics from exercise 1 are mentioned? Where is each conversation taking place?

|   | Topic(s) | Place |
|---|---|---|
| 1 |  |  |
| 2 |  |  |
| 3 |  |  |

AUDIO
26–28

**3** Complete the sentences from the dialogues with words from the box. Then listen again to check your answers.

> about • all • based • checking • do • excuse me • from • join •
> looking after • mind • near • noticing • so • sorry • way • with

1  I'm _____, but I couldn't help _____ you've got a Chipper bag.

2  I'm Ute Adena, by the _____.

3  What company are you _____?

4  _____, do you know if this is the stop for the CASPA trade fair?

5  I'm _____ Germany, _____ Frankfurt …

6  So, are you _____ a stand at the fair?

7  Where are you _____?

8  And what _____ you? What _____ you do?

9  Excuse me, do you _____ if I _____ you?

10  Not at _____.

11  _____, when did you get here?

12  That sounds like something worth _____ out.

**Which of the sentences 1–12 are used to ...**

a   start a conversation?  _____

b   react?  _____

c   find out more information?  _____

---

**SAFE SMALL-TALK TOPICS**

Here is a general guide to which small-talk topics are safe and which are unsafe.

**very safe**                                                                                                   **unsafe**

| THE WEATHER | TRAVEL | SPORT | WORK | FAMILY | MONEY | POLITICS | RELIGION |
|---|---|---|---|---|---|---|---|

Of course, safe small-talk topics differ between countries, and also between people. For example, money is a more common small-talk topic in the US than in the UK. And religion can be a very 'dangerous' topic in the US and the UK. If you're not sure which topics are safe, the best thing is to stay with the very safe topics until the other person introduces other topics.

---

**4**   **Choose one line from each column to make mini-dialogues.**

| Person A | Person B | Person A |
|---|---|---|
| 1   I'm James, by the way. | a   Jitterbug Software. We make computer games. | A   Well, let's hope the shuttle comes soon! |
| 2   So, what company are you with? | b   I think so! I need to go there too. | B   We're based in Birmingham. |
| 3   Where are you based? | c   No, never. I'd like to go there one day though. | C   Thanks. I really need a break! |
| 4   When did you get here? | d   Nice to meet you. I'm Susan. | D   I arrived late last night. |
| 5   So, are you working on one of the stands? | e   Just this morning. What about you? When did you come? | E   You should if you get the chance. It's very beautiful. |
| 6   Excuse me, do you know if this is the bus stop for the trade fair? | f   In Linz, in Austria. And your company? | F   Me too. |
| 7   Do you mind if I join you? | g   No, not at all. Take a seat. | G   Ah, OK. I think I know the name. |
| 8   Have you ever been to Switzerland? | h   No, I'm just here to look around. | H   Nice to meet you too. |

**5**    **Work with a partner. Use the information in the Partner Files to role-play conversations that take place at a trade fair. Try to use phrases from the Language Box below.**

**STRIKING UP A CONVERSATION**

Excuse me, are you …?
I noticed that …
I'm [*name*], by the way.
Have you seen this before?

**PARTNER FILES**    Partner A    File 6, p. 61
Partner B    File 6, p. 63

AUDIO

29

**6**    **Ute is talking to a potential supplier, Thomas Vogt from Xene Electronics, at his stand. Listen and answer the questions below.**

1    What does Thomas want to show Ute?
2    Why does Ute have to go?
3    When does Ute say she will see the product?
4    Do you think Ute will really come back to the stand?

**7**    **Order the words to make sentences from the dialogue.**

1    probably / kind / I should / that's very / but / get going / of you /.

_____

2    only / it'll / a minute / take /.

_____

3    meeting someone / supposed / actually / in ten minutes / I'm / to be /.

_____

4    a couple / you're / they won't mind / I'm sure / if / late / of minutes /.

_____

5    afterwards / a look / come back / why don't I / to take / ?

_____

6    afraid / really / go / I'm / should / I /.

_____

7    right back / my appointment / come / I'll / after /.

_____

8    then / a little while / you / see / in /.

_____

**Who says which sentences above?**

Ute:  *1,*  _____          Thomas:  _____

---

**ENDING A CONVERSATION POLITELY**

Sometimes it can be difficult to end a conversation politely. Here are some tips for getting away from people without being rude.

- Exchange business cards (this is often a signal you want to end the conversation):

    *Anyway, let me give you my card.*
    *Listen, do you have a card?*

- Say you have to leave because of another commitment, e.g. another meeting:
    *Sorry, I really have to go now. My boss is waiting for me outside.*
    *I should really get going. I have another appointment in a couple of minutes.*

- Say you've seen someone you want to talk to:
    *Listen, I've just seen Chris over there. Excuse me a moment, I really need to catch him.*

Native speakers often use words like *so*, *right then*, and *OK* (often with the person's name) to signal that they are ready to finish the conversation. The sentence 'It was nice talking to you' is a very clear signal that the person wants to move on.

---

**8**  **Rewrite B's lines to make them more polite.**

1   A   Can I show you our latest product?
    B   ~~No. I have to go. Goodbye.~~

    *Sorry. I'd love to see it, but I should really get going.*

2   A   Let me get you another coffee.
    B   ~~No, thanks. I'm going to talk to my friend over there.~~

    _____

3   A   Have you seen our new brochure?
    B   ~~No. I have another appointment now.~~

    _____

4   A   Let me introduce you to Sandra, our marketing assistant.
    B   ~~I don't have time. My boss is waiting for me.~~

    _____

5   A   Let me demonstrate our latest software.
    B   ~~Here's my card. I have to go. Call me next week.~~

    _____

**9**  **Work with a partner. Use the profiles in the Partner Files to role-play ending a conversation politely.**

**PARTNER FILES**  Partner A   File 7, p. 61
Partner B   File 7, p. 63

AUDIO
30–35

**10** Read this short article from a management publication. Then listen to six extracts from trade fair conversations (a–f) and match them to the strategies (1–6).

---

# *BORED* with typical small talk questions?

> Are you bored with small talk? When you're at a trade fair and have had the same conversation with 20 different people, you don't want to hear the question 'Is this your first time in …?' again. And, more importantly, you won't develop those key business relationships if your conversation partner thinks you're boring.

So it's time to get interesting! Here are some strategies that you can use when people aren't interested in the usual small talk questions.

**1** Give your (strong) opinion on something connected to the trade fair or situation.

**2** Make a joke about something.

**3** Talk about something funny that has happened to you during the trade fair (or at another trade fair).

**4** Open up to someone by telling them something personal.

**5** Show your partner an object you've picked up at the trade fair.

**6** Make an interesting observation.

---

| Extract | Strategy | Extract | Strategy |
|---------|----------|---------|----------|
| a | 2 | d | ☐ |
| b | ☐ | e | ☐ |
| c | ☐ | f | ☐ |

Choose three of the strategies above and think of something you can say for each one.
Then work with a partner (imagine you are both at a trade fair or another event)
and make a dialogue using the three strategies you have chosen.

AUDIO
30–35

**11**  **Complete these sentences from the dialogues with words from the box. Then listen again to check your answers.**

> amazes • ever • experience • hand out • hate • imagine • keep • look • weird

1  I've only managed to _____ three business cards.

2  _____ at this amazing pen …

3  It always _____ me at trade fairs how …

4  Isn't that _____?

5  I had this really strange _____ earlier today.

6  Can you _____?

7  This is really the worst-organized trade fair I've _____ seen.

8  I'm sorry I _____ looking at my phone.

9  I _____ being away from home when my kids are ill.

**12**  **Work with a partner to make small talk during a coffee break.**

**A**

> Ask **B** if he/she is enjoying the trade fair.

> Comment on the free gift. Give a strong opinion about something connected to the trade fair.

> React. Give some personal information about yourself.

**B**

> Respond. 'Show' **A** a free gift you got at a stand.

> React to **A**'s opinion. Give some personal information about yourself.

> End the conversation politely.

---

**SMALL TALK AT A TRADE FAIR**

**Showing someone an object**
Look at this … I got it at the … stand.
Look what they gave me at the … stand.
That's really cool/interesting/amazing.
**Giving an opinion**
I always think that …
It always surprises me that …
The thing about trade fairs is …
**Giving personal information**
I need to call my husband/wife/son/daughter later.
My … is ill/on holiday/at work.
I talked to my … yesterday and he/she said …

**13** Ute has written a follow-up email to a potential supplier that she met at the trade fair. Complete her email using the phrases below.

a   do you mind if I ask
b   enjoyed hearing about
c   hope to see you
d   in advance
e   put me in touch

f   talking to them
g   told our head of department
h   very nice to meet you
i   you could send him
j   you mentioned

---

**From:** 'Ute Adena' ute.adena@pixdorf.de    **To:** 'Yves Montrand' yves.montrand@pleinair.fr

**Subject:**   Nice to meet you

Dear Yves

I just wanted to say it was _____ [1] at the trade fair last week. I _____ [2]
your products and the markets you operate in. I _____ [3] about your inventory software
and he is interested in learning more about it. Do you think _____ [4] some information?
His name is Dieter Steinmetz and his email is dieter.steinmetz@pixdorf.de.

By the way, _____ [5] that your company works closely together with GroupSoft. I'm
interested in _____ [6] about a possible project – _____ [7] who your contact
person there is? I'd be very grateful if you could _____ [8] with someone there. Thanks
_____ [9]!

Take care, and _____ [10] again soon!

Best wishes

Ute

---

**Now write Ute's follow-up email to Per Jensen (see exercise 2, track 28).**

| FOLLOW-UP EMAILS |
| --- |

It is a good idea to write a follow-up email to people you have met at a trade fair when you are
back in the office. That way you can keep in touch and make sure they remember who you are.
It's best if you have a concrete question or proposal in your email; that way they are sure to
answer you, helping to build the relationship. Here are some useful phrases:

*I just wanted to ask/mention/send …*
*Here is the information we talked about …*
*I'd be interested in learning more/hearing about …*
*Could you put me in touch with …?*

**OUTPUT** Read the article and answer the questions which follow.

# How to tell a story or an anecdote in English

One of the hardest skills in a foreign language (or in our first language, for that matter) is telling an interesting story or anecdote. Learners of English often feel left out when socializing with groups of native speakers and everyone else is telling stories except them. It's a good skill to learn – everyone likes to listen to stories and a good storyteller quickly becomes the centre of any group. And talking about your experiences is one of the best ways to build up a relationship with someone.

Fortunately there are some easy ways to make your anecdotes livelier and more enjoyable to listen to. Here are some tips which will make it easier for you to tell stories and anecdotes in English.

## Make that link

Try to connect your story to what people are already talking about. There's nothing more boring than a story which is not connected somehow to the present conversation. And it also gives the impression that the storyteller hasn't been listening. On the other hand, a story which illustrates a point you are talking about can be a very powerful rhetorical technique. Use a phrase like 'That reminds me of something that happened to me' or 'It's funny you should say that because something similar happened to me' to make the connection to your story and begin telling it.

## Stay in the present

Use the present tense ('So I say to him …') instead of the past ('So I said to him …'). Not only is the grammar easier, it makes your story more direct and alive. It is very common for native speakers of English to tell stories in the present tense.

## Why not use rhetorical questions?

Use rhetorical questions like 'So do you know what I do next?' or 'And what does she say?' to create suspense and variety.

## Get emotional

Talk about what you thought and how you felt at different points in the story ('So there I am in the airport, all alone and feeling like a complete idiot, wishing I'd stayed at home'). It gives the story 'colour' and helps the listener identify with what you are describing.

## Use your voice

Vary your voice as much as possible to keep the listener interested: speak slowly or fast, quietly or loudly, in different accents (if you can!). And use timing well – there's nothing more dramatic than a long pause at the most exciting part of the story ('And do you know what was in the box …?'). ■

AUDIO

36

**OVER TO YOU**

- First listen to this example anecdote. Which tips from the article does the speaker use?
- Now think of something interesting that happened to you or someone you know. Write out the story exactly as you would tell it. Show it to your partner or teacher. Do they have any ideas for making it better? Then tell your anecdote to the other students. Try to tell the story without looking at your text.

# Test yourself!

**See how much you've learned about socializing in English. Use the clues to complete the crossword puzzle.**

## Across

1 Another word for *talked about*: *You … your mother-in-law earlier.*

4 Another way to say *collect*: *I'll … you … at about seven.* (two words – 4, 2)

7 One way to take your coffee: *Just …, thanks.*

9 Another way to say *I'm sorry*: *… , I just don't have time today.* (two words – 2, 6)

11 *It's great to finally m_ _ _ you.*

14 *This trade fair is so much better than the … one.*

15 Another word for *relatives*: *I have … in Australia.*

17 Another word for *hear*: *I didn't quite … that.*

18 What's the preposition? *I look forward … seeing you on Tuesday.*

19 What's the preposition? *It's the second door … the left.*

20 Another way to say *in fact*: *I … learned Spanish at school.*

22 *I live in New York City, so I m_ _ _ the countryside sometimes.*

24 Another word for *very hungry*: *I'm absolutely … .*

25 *Can I g _ _ you a coffee?*

26 Another word for *out of work*: *Before I got this job I was … for two years.*

29 Another word for *very cold*: *It was … in Scotland when I left.*

## Down

2 *I work in the purchasing d_ _ _ _ _ _ _ _ _ .*

3 *The meeting should only t_ _ _ an hour.*

5 Another word for *nice*: *That's very … of you.*

6 Another way to say *meet us* or *come with us*: *I was wondering if you might like to … for dinner tonight.* (two words – 4, 2)

7 Another way to say *incidentally*: *I'm Ute Adena, b_ t_ _ w_ _.*

8 *I think I'll have the pasta for my m_ _ _ c_ _ _ _ _.*

10 Another American English word for *bathroom*: *Is there a … around here?*

12 Another way to say *leave*: *I should probably … .* (2 words – 3, 5)

13 Another way to say *in the past*: *I … live in Sweden.* (2 words – 4, 2)

14 Another word for *place*: *Have you been in this … long?*

16 *I live in Barcelona, but I'm from London o_ _ _ _ _ _ _ _ _.*

21 [*In a restaurant*]: *That was a lovely meal. Shall we get the … ?*

23 Another word for *employees*: *How many members of … do you have here?*

27 *There's a nice e_ _ _ _ _ _ _ _ on at the art gallery at the moment.*

28 What's the preposition? *Shall we get … to business?*

# Partner Files

### Role-play 1

Chris/Christine: You are meeting Robert/Roberta Brown, a supplier from Britain, at the airport in Frankfurt. You have never met before but have spoken a lot over the phone. Robert/Roberta is carrying several heavy bags. Greet him/her and ask about the flight. Make some small talk (weather, plans for today) and take him/her to your car/a taxi.

### Role-play 2

Michael/Michelle: You are visiting the Dutch subsidiary of your company. A colleague there – Daniel/Daniella – is meeting you at the station in Amsterdam. You've met before. Your train was delayed by twenty minutes. There were no services on the train and you would like to buy a bottle of water before you go to the company.

You are visiting a company and are in the meeting room. You want to know how to get to different places in the building. Ask your partner for directions to the kitchen, Sue's office and the reception area, and mark them on your plan. Then change roles. When you have finished, check your partner's plan to make sure you gave him/her the right directions.

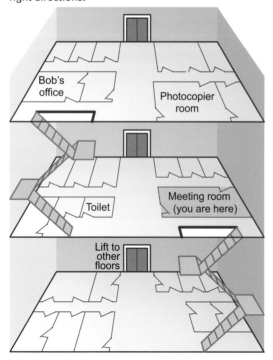

You are visiting one of your customers at his/her company. You have been working together for several years and you know a lot of the same people. Ask your partner about his/her two colleagues below. How are they and what are they doing?
- Hilda Pearson
- John Young

Your partner will ask you about these people, who work at your company. (Complete the gaps below before starting the role-play.)

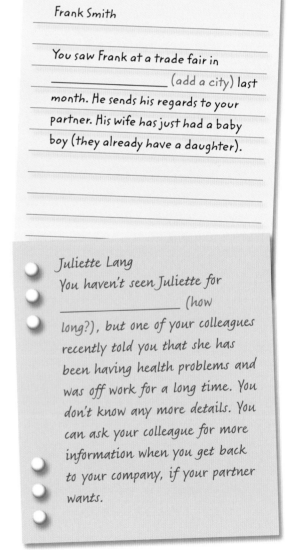

Frank Smith

You saw Frank at a trade fair in _____ (add a city) last month. He sends his regards to your partner. His wife has just had a baby boy (they already have a daughter).

Juliette Lang
You haven't seen Juliette for _____ (how long?), but one of your colleagues recently told you that she has been having health problems and was off work for a long time. You don't know any more details. You can ask your colleague for more information when you get back to your company, if your partner wants.

**UNIT 4, EXERCISE 13**   **FILE 4**

You are looking after a visitor to your town/city. You would like to spend as much time with your business contact as possible. Here are some places you could visit with him/her. Make suggestions about what to do.

**City Leisure Centre**

Has a huge swimming pool with slides and wave machine. Also squash and badminton courts.

**'Hochfeld'**

Traditional Swiss restaurant – specializes in cheese dishes – 30 minutes' drive from the city.

**Renaissance Theatre**

Has a version of 'Hamlet' at the moment which is supposed to be very good. The play is four hours long.

**Bohemian Café**

Historic café built in 1920. One of the big tourist sights in your city. Specializes in cocktails.

**UNIT 5, EXERCISE 11**   **FILE 5**

You are having dinner in a restaurant with an important business partner. (You are the guest.) Ask your partner questions to keep the conversation going.

Here are some things your partner mentioned earlier:
- He/She plays badminton in her free time.
- He/She has an adopted son.
- His/Her mother is visiting at the moment.

Begin by asking your partner a question about the restaurant.

**UNIT 6, EXERCISE 5**   **FILE 6**

**Role-play 1**

You are standing in the queue to get a coffee at the trade fair café. There are lots of people in front of you and the queue is moving very slowly. However, you have an hour before your next appointment and you are not in a hurry. Start a conversation with the person next to you. You see from their badge that they work for a company which is a potential client for you. Find out who they are and what their position in the company is.

**Role-play 2**

You work for a company called Tiramax. You are visiting the stand of your competitor Misuto to see which new products they have. They have a very interesting new scanner. Speak to the person on the stand and do the following things:
- Try to find out as much information about the new product as you can.
- Also, try to find out what the company's future plans are.
- Invite the person to go for a coffee so you can talk to them for longer.

**UNIT 6, EXERCISE 9**   **FILE 7**

You are at your company's stand at a trade fair. You are talking to one of your most important clients. It's important to build the relationship and you have to keep the conversation going. Don't let them get away!

# Partner Files

## UNIT 1, EXERCISE 5        FILE 1

### Role-play 1
Robert/Roberta: You have just arrived at the airport in Frankfurt and have made arrangements for your business partner, Chris/Christine, to pick you up. You have spoken a lot over the phone but have never met before. You are carrying several heavy bags. Your flight was fine and you had a DVD to watch. You would like to use the toilet before leaving the airport.

### Role-play 2
Daniel/Daniella: You are picking Michael/Michelle up at the station in Amsterdam. He/She works for the European division of your company and you have met him/her before. The train was delayed by twenty minutes.

## UNIT 2, EXERCISE 9        FILE 2

You are visiting a company and are in the meeting room. You want to know how to get to different places in the building. Ask your partner for directions to Bob's office, the toilet and the photocopier room, and mark them on your plan. Then change roles. When you have finished, check your partner's plan to make sure you gave him/her the right directions.

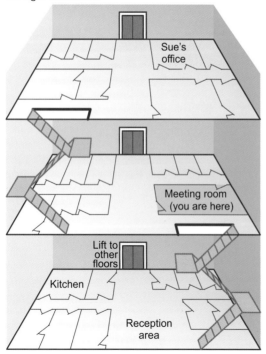

## UNIT 3, EXERCISE 4        FILE 3

One of your suppliers is visiting you at your company. You have been working together for several years and you know a lot of the same people. Ask your partner about his/her two colleagues below. How are they and what are they doing?
• Frank Smith
• Juliette Lang

Your partner will ask you about these people, who work at your company. (Complete the gaps below before starting the role-play.)

Hilda Pearson

Hilda left your company two months ago. You think she has gone to work for a company in _____ _____ (add a city), but you are not sure.
You have her new email address in your office, if your partner would like to contact her.

John Young

You have been working a lot with John on a project recently. He is very busy at the moment and quite stressed. He's going on holiday to _____ (add a country) next week and you think he needs a rest.

## UNIT 4, EXERCISE 13 — FILE 4

You are visiting an important business contact in another town/city. You would like to spend time with him/her, but you have a lot of things to think about today:

- You have an important presentation to prepare for tomorrow. It will take at least two hours to prepare.
- Today is your son's birthday. You have to phone home this evening to wish him a happy birthday.
- You hurt your knee playing squash last week and you can't sit for long or walk far.

Your partner will invite you to do different things. Respond to his/her invitations. Don't forget the things you have to do today. At the same time, remember that this is an important business relationship and that you have to accept at least one invitation!

## UNIT 5, EXERCISE 11 — FILE 5

You are having dinner in a restaurant with an important business partner. (You are the host.) Ask your partner questions to keep the conversation going.

Here are some things your partner mentioned earlier:

- He/She has recently bought a new house.
- His/Her partner has a new job.
- He/She wants to go to Italy on holiday this year.

Begin by saying something about the food.

## UNIT 6, EXERCISE 5 — FILE 6

**Role-play 1**

You are standing in the queue to get a coffee at the trade fair café. There are lots of people in front of you and the queue is moving very slowly. You have just given a presentation about one of your company's products to a group of 100 people and are feeling very tired. You really need to sit down and relax. However, your presentation went well and you feel satisfied with it. Lots of people talked to you after the presentation and asked for more information about the product.

**Role-play 2**

You work for a company called Misuto, which you are representing at a trade fair. The person next to you is looking at one of your new products, a scanner. You worked on the project and are very pleased with the product, which is the most modern scanner of its kind on the market. Start a conversation with the person and do the following things:

- Tell them about the new scanner.
- Find out as much information as you can about the person. Are they a potential customer?

## UNIT 6, EXERCISE 9 — FILE 7

You are at the stand of one of your suppliers at a trade fair, talking to your contact person there. You are going to change to another supplier soon and you are not interested in talking to the person (who you think is very boring anyway!). Try to get away from them as soon as you can. Use any excuse you can think of!

# Answer key

**page 6**

**1** a is the most formal, b the least

|  | more formal | less formal |
|---|---|---|
| salutation | Dear … | Hi … |
| fixed phrases | Thank you<br>I would be delighted regarding your forthcoming visit | Thanks |
| closing | I look forward to<br>Kind regards | Looking forward to<br>All the best |

**2** 1 c    2 a    3 b

**page 7**

1 Have the speakers met before?
 **1** no
 **2** no
 **3** yes

2 Is the conversation formal or informal?
 **1** informal
 **2** formal
 **3** informal

3 Where are they meeting?
 **1** at the airport
 **2** at the airport
 **3** at Paul's company

4 What problems did the visitors have during the journey?
 **1** flight was long and the speaker didn't have enough legroom
 **2** there was some turbulence over the North Sea
 **3** the traffic was terrible (only one lane open over the bridge)

5 What are they doing next?
 **1** Alison wants to go to the toilet to wash her hands
 **2** Ms Janiak will take Mr Syms to his hotel
 **3** they will go to Paul's office

**3** 1 must
 2 finally, person
 3 hope, waiting
 4 pleasure
 5 flight
 6 see, again
 7 waiting
 8 help, bags
 9 mind

a 1, 2, 4, 6
b 5
c 8, 9
d 3, 7

**page 8**

**4** 1 f
 2 e
 3 a, c, h, k
 4 a, c, d, h, k
 5 a, c, d, h
 6 g
 7 g, j
 8 b, i

**page 9**

**6** The topic is the weather.
 1 sunny
 2 weather
 3 raining
 4 terrible
 5 lucky
 6 warm
 7 hot
 8 cold
 9 down
 10 wet

**page 10**

**7**

| words describing temperature | words describing the sky | words to do with water |
|---|---|---|
| *cold*<br>freezing<br>mild<br>roasting<br>warm | *cloudy*<br>grey<br>hazy<br>overcast<br>sunny | *damp*<br>drizzling<br>humid<br>pouring<br>rainy |

**8** (suggested answers)
*11:40 Mr Syms arrives at Warsaw airport, flight BA120*
*12 (approx)* lunch – *Il Casolare*
2 p.m. meeting with sales team
4 p.m. visit to production plant
5 p.m. Mr Syms back to hotel by taxi
7 p.m. pick Mr Syms up for dinner

**page 11**

**9** 1 not far, there
 2 check into, drop off
 3 can grab, near
 4 can go
 5 have the meeting
 6 're going to visit
 7 should only take
 8 can take, relax
 9 'll pick you up
 10 should be, 're going

**page 12**

**11 Across**
 3 get
 5 pleasure
 6 pick
 7 should
 9 waiting
 10 just
 11 restroom
 12 delighted

**Down**
 1 freezing
 2 come
 4 great
 5 pouring
 8 bags
 10 journey

The mystery phrase is *small talk*.

**page 14**

**1** The topics discussed include the journey, the offices and the company.

**page 15**

1 Sanne Heitink.
2 No, they haven't.
3 So that she can leave her briefcase and coat there.
4 Six months.
5 It is bright and airy.
6 Ten years ago.
7 31.
8 (A cup of) coffee.

**2** 1 Did you have any trouble finding us?
2 The directions on your website were very clear.
3 You can leave your briefcase and coat in my office.
4 I'll take you round to meet a few members of the team.
5 Would you like something to drink?
6 A cup of coffee would be great.

### page 16

**3**

| talking about the building | talking about the company and its history |
|---|---|
| *(ground/first/second) floor* | *department* |
| lift | employees |
| location | to expand |
| to move into | to be founded |
| neighbourhood | to restructure |
| reception | staff |
| stairs | to own |
| facilities | |

1 location/neighbourhood
2 moved into
3 neighbourhood/location
4 founded
5 employees
6 expanded
7 floor
8 lift

### page 17

**4** 1 e
2 g
3 b
4 a
5 c
6 f
7 d

a Always a pleasure./It's the least I could do./You're welcome.
b After you.
c Here we are.
d Here you are.
e Thank you.

### page 18

**5** 1 e
2 d
3 f
4 c, d
5 b, c
6 a, b

### page 19

**7** 1 down, on
2 where
3 by
4 On
5 out of, into
6 when, first
7 back

**8** 2 kitchen
3 lifts
4 toilet
5 photocopier

### page 20

**10** 1 marketing manager
2 Mary (Chan)
3 assistant (to product designer)
4 Emin (Murat)

**11** 1 f   2 c   3 a   4 h   5 g
6 b   7 e   8 d

### page 21

**12** 1 catch
2 say
3 Sorry
4 sure
5 follow
6 meant
7 see
8 could
9 again
10 are

**UNIT 3**

### page 23

**1** 1 Anja left the company last July.
2 She lives in Utrecht now.
3 She's working as a designer for a bicycle manufacturer.
4 Chris is now the product manager.
5 He doesn't often go to trade fairs any more. / He's in the office more.

### page 24

**2** 1 d   E
2 e   B
3 c   A
4 a   D
5 b   C

**3** 1 Not to worry.
2 That's good to hear.
3 I can imagine.
4 How's he doing these days?
5 He says hello, by the way.

### page 25

**5**

| Sport | Relaxing at home |
|---|---|
| skiing | listening to music |
| doing yoga | reading |
| keeping fit | watching television |
| playing football | cooking |

**Going out**
eating out
going to the cinema
shopping
going to concerts

**6** 1 go
2 playing
3 Have, done
4 do, go
5 have played/have been playing
6 went
7 do
8 do

### page 27

**8** 1 Mary
2 Sanne
3 José Maria
4 Sanne
5 Sanne (and her husband
6 Valérie

**9** 1 Shall we, say
2 Can I get
3 would be great
4 Can I use
5 Here's, Just
6 got there
7 if you like
8 first time
9 or pleasure
10 ever been

### page 28

**10** 2 – g – F
3 – a – G
4 – b – D
5 – f – A
6 – c – B
7 – d – E

### page 29

**12** b  J
c  S
d  J
e  S
f  S

1  c
2  e
3  a
4  f
5  d
6  b

## UNIT 4

### page 31

1 Conversation 1     E (cathedral)
  Conversation 2     B (castle)
  Conversation 3     C (art gallery)

  1 The cathedral was built in the 16th century (not the 15th).
  2 The castle was built by King Heinrich the First (not by King Heinrich the Second).
  3 The brewery closed in 1994 (not in 1992).

### page 32

2 1 This
  2 typical
  3 telling
  4 built
  5 destroyed
  6 building
  7 shut
  8 supposed

### page 33

4 My town/city has a(n) airport/castle/cathedral/ conference centre/harbour/university.
  It's a(n) beautiful/historic/important/industrial/ large/small town/city.
  It's a bit bigger than/about the same size as/much smaller than/close to/near Oxford/London.
  It's the national/regional/state capital.
  It's close to/near the Czech Republic/France.
  It's close to/near/on the Danube/Rhine.

### page 34

6 1 False. Cristina is from a little village just outside Milano.
  2 False. She went to university in Torino.
  3 True.
  4 False. Sharon doesn't want to leave town in case she misses her flight.
  5 False. It's an antiques fair.

### page 35

7 1 c    2 g    3 b    4 e    5 a    6 h    7 f    8 d

### page 36

9 1 country
  2 nice
  3 free
  4 recommendations
  5 museum
  6 take
  7 fair
  8 really
  9 sounds, love
  10 pick, Say

The host says: 1, 5, 6, 7, 8, 10
The guest says: 2, 3, 4, 9

### page 37

11

|   | 1 | 2 | 3 | 4 |
|---|---|---|---|---|
| a | to go for dinner tonight | to meet for coffee next week | to go to the opera tonight | to come to host's party on Saturday |
| b | accepts | turns down | turns down | accepts |
| c |  | away at a trade fair next week | meeting a friend for dinner |  |
| d |  | meeting the week after that | going next time host is going |  |

1 I was wondering if you would like to join us for dinner tonight?
2 How about meeting for a coffee next week?
3 I have an extra ticket for the opera tonight.
4 Would you like to come?
5 My partner and I are having a party next Saturday.
6 We were hoping you could come.

### page 38

12 (suggested answers)
  2 That sounds nice, but I'm afraid I'm quite busy today. How about tomorrow?
  3 I'd love to, but I'm afraid I have to prepare a presentation for tomorrow. Maybe you'd like to come over for dinner next week?
  4 That's very nice of you, but I've actually arranged to meet someone else tonight. Maybe we can go for a drink some time next week.

## UNIT 5

### page 41

1 See Transcript on page 71.

2 2 g    3 h    4 f    5 a    6 d    7 j    8 c    9 b    10 e

### page 42

3 1 fondue     2 lasagne     3 curry

4

| parts of the meal | types of meat | types of vegetable |
|---|---|---|
| *dessert* starter/ appetizer main course | *beef* pork chicken ham lamb | pepper onion cabbage courgette/ zucchini |
| **side dishes** | **ways of cooking** | **words for describing food** |
| rice potato wedges salad chips/French fries | bake roast grill/broil fry | sweet rich savoury light spicy |

### page 43

6 They talk about the following topics:
the restaurant, holidays, family, sport.

1 did you like
2 tasty, perfectly
3 you come here
4 about you
5 are you married as
6 mentioned your mother-in-law
7 went to Croatia last summer
8 you do any sports
9 were saying you went
10 Talking of, dessert

### page 44

7 1 divorced
   married
   separated
   single
  2 relations
   relatives
  3 a acquaintance     c only child
   b mother-in-law     d step-son
  4 is having/is going to have/is expecting
  5 brother-in-law
  6 wives/partners
  7 girlfriend
  8 only children

**page 45**

**9** (model answers)

2 She's six. Actually she recently started school. What about you? Do you have any children?

3 An Alsatian. He's great fun but he needs lots of exercise! Do you have any pets?

4 Six years. I joined straight after university. And what about you? Have you been with your company long?

5 Yes, I have. I was there three years ago, on business. Have you ever been there?

6 I play squash. I meet my friends once a week for a game. And you? Do you play any sports?

7 No, it's not. It's very hot for us. It's usually about 25 degrees in the summer. What's the weather like where you live?

**page 46**

**10**

| | | | | | |
|---|---|---|---|---|---|
| 2 | b | 4 | a | 6 | g |
| 3 | c, e, f | 5 | d | 7 | e |

We say *that must be* … when commenting on present situations, and *that must have been* … when commenting on past situations.

**12** 1 True.
2 False. Only Carlo wants one.
3 True.
4 False
5 True.

**page 47**

**13** 1 get
2 catch
3 get
4 's
5 're
6 put
7 round
8 have

## UNIT 6

**page 49**

**1** 1 companies
2 practical information (transport)
3 the weather
4 hotel
5 exhibits
6 the trade fair
7 home town/country

**page 50**

**2**

| | Topic(s) | Place |
|---|---|---|
| 1 | companies, hotel | at the hotel |
| 2 | practical information, weather, home country, the trade fair, companies | at a bus stop |
| 3 | practical information, the trade fair, exhibits | in a café at the trade fair |

**3** 1 sorry, noticing
2 way
3 with
4 Excuse me
5 from, near
6 looking after
7 based
8 about, do
9 mind, join
10 all
11 So
12 checking

**page 51**

a 1, 2, 4, 5, 9    b 10, 12    c 3, 6, 7, 8, 11

**4** 2 – a – G
3 – f – B
4 – e – D
5 – h – F
6 – b – A
7 – g – C
8 – c – E

**page 52**

**6** 1 Their new wireless printer.
2 She has another appointment in ten minutes.
3 Right after her appointment.
4 Probably not!

**7** 1 That's very kind of you, but I should probably get going.
2 It'll only take a minute.
3 I'm actually supposed to be meeting someone in ten minutes.
4 I'm sure they won't mind if you're a couple of minutes late.
5 Why don't I come back afterwards to take a look?
6 I'm afraid I really should go.
7 I'll come right back after my appointment.
8 See you in a little while then.

Ute: 1, 3, 5, 6, 7, 8
Thomas: 2, 4

**page 53**

**8** (suggested answers)
2 That would be nice, but I've just seen someone I really need to talk to over there.
3 Actually, I should get going. I have another appointment in a few minutes.
4 I'm really sorry, but I don't really have time at the moment. My boss is waiting for me, I'm afraid.
5 I'm sorry. I really have to go now. Let me give you my card. Perhaps you could call me next week.

**page 54**

**10** a 2    b 5    c 6    d 3    e 1    f 4

**page 55**

**11** 1 hand out
2 Look
3 amazes
4 weird
5 experience
6 imagine
7 ever
8 keep
9 hate

**page 56**

**13** 1 h    2 b    3 g    4 i    5 j
6 f    7 a    8 e    9 d    10 c

**pages 58–59**

**Test yourself!**

| *Across* | *Down* |
|---|---|
| 1 mentioned | 2 department |
| 4 pick up | 3 take |
| 7 black | 5 kind |
| 9 I'm afraid | 6 join us |
| 11 meet | 7 by the way |
| 14 last | 8 main course |
| 15 relations | 10 restroom |
| 17 catch | 12 get going |
| 18 to | 13 used to |
| 19 on | 14 location |
| 20 actually | 16 originally |
| 22 miss | 21 bill |
| 24 starving | 22 staff |
| 25 get | 27 exhibition |
| 26 unemployed | 28 down |
| 29 freezing | |

# Transcripts

**Dialogue 1**

| | |
|---|---|
| *Raj* | Alison Taylor? |
| *Alison* | That's me. You must be Raj. |
| *Raj* | Yes, that's right. Hello! It's great to finally meet you in person after all our phone calls and emails. |
| *Alison* | Yes, I know. I hope you haven't been waiting long. |
| *Raj* | No, I just got here ten minutes ago. So, how was the flight? |
| *Alison* | Long! Since the budget cuts, we've had to fly economy and, I must say, I miss the legroom. |
| *Raj* | Tell me about it. Have the airlines forgotten that people are a lot taller now than they were 20 years ago? |
| *Alison* | Yes, indeed. And we're also quite a bit wider than we were 20 years ago! |
| *Raj* | Right. |
| *Alison* | At least I had an exit row seat. Anyway, I'd just like to wash my hands before we get going. Is there a toilet somewhere? |
| *Raj* | Yes, there's one just this way … |

**Dialogue 2**

| | |
|---|---|
| *Kasia* | Mr Syms? Hello, I'm Kasia Janiak from BTO Systems. Welcome to Warsaw. |
| *Mr Syms* | Hello, Ms Janiak. It's a pleasure to meet you. |
| *Kasia* | A pleasure to meet you, too. How was your flight? |
| *Mr Syms* | Uneventful, thankfully. There was some turbulence over the North Sea, but otherwise no difficulties. |
| *Kasia* | I'm glad to hear it. So, if you'll just come this way … . The taxi is over here. I'll accompany you to your hotel. |
| *Mr Syms* | Wonderful. Is the hotel far from here? |
| *Kasia* | No, not at all. About twenty minutes or so. |

**Dialogue 3**

| | |
|---|---|
| *Anna* | Hi, Paul, good to see you again. |
| *Paul* | Hi, Anna, good to see you too. |
| *Anna* | Sorry to keep you waiting. The train was on time but the traffic here is terrible. There was only one lane open over the bridge so the traffic was really slow. The taxi driver said it's been like that for weeks. |
| *Paul* | I know, the traffic here is a complete nightmare. I should have told you to take the ring road. Sorry, I completely forgot about that. Anyway, can I help you with your bags? |
| *Anna* | That would be great. Would you mind taking this? It's the projector for this afternoon's presentation. |
| *Paul* | Not at all. So, my office is just over here … |

| | |
|---|---|
| *Mr Syms* | I can't believe it's so sunny here. It makes a nice change from England! |
| *Kasia* | How was the weather when you left? |
| *Mr Syms* | It was raining, as usual! This summer has been terrible. |
| *Kasia* | Well, we've been very lucky here. The last couple of weeks have been very warm. |
| *Mr Syms* | Do you normally get good summers here? |
| *Kasia* | It depends. Usually we get at least a few hot days, but sometimes it rains a lot. |
| *Mr Syms* | I imagine the winters here must be pretty cold. |
| *Kasia* | Oh yes. Sometimes it goes down to minus 15. |
| *Mr Syms* | Well, at least it never gets that cold in England. The winter there is usually just grey and wet. It can be quite depressing! |
| *Kasia* | Ugh! Well, I'm glad the weather is nice for your visit here … |

| | |
|---|---|
| *Kasia* | It's not far now. We'll be there in five minutes. |
| *Mr Syms* | Great. |
| *Kasia* | So, I thought you might like to check into your hotel first and drop off your things. Then we can grab a spot of lunch. There's a nice Italian place near your hotel. |
| *Mr Syms* | Sounds good! |
| *Kasia* | After that we can go to the office. We have the meeting with the sales team at two, as you know. |
| *Mr Syms* | Yes, that should be interesting. |
| *Kasia* | At four we're going to visit the production plant. |
| *Mr Syms* | Right. |
| *Kasia* | That should only take an hour. Then perhaps you can take a taxi back to your hotel and relax for a bit. I'll pick you up again at about seven for dinner. |
| *Mr Syms* | Oh yes, it's the big company dinner tonight, isn't it? |
| *Kasia* | Exactly. It should be really good. We're going to this fantastic French restaurant. The food there is amazing! |

| | |
|---|---|
| *J. María* | Hello, Ms Heitink. I'm José María Molinero. Welcome to Salas Design. |
| *Sanne* | It's very nice to meet you. Please, call me Sanne. |
| *J. María* | And I'm José María. It's not a girl's name, as you know! |
| *Sanne* | No, I know. People have trouble with my name as well. It's got two syllables: sah-na. |
| *J. María* | Right. So did you have any trouble finding us? |
| *Sanne* | No, not at all. The directions on your website were very clear. |
| *J. María* | Glad to hear it. So, if you'll just come this way, Sanne … . You can leave your briefcase and coat in my office, and then I'll take you round to meet a few members of the team. They're all looking forward to meeting you. |

| | |
|---|---|
| Sanne | Great, me too. ... This is a lovely space you have here. Have you been in this location long? |
| J. María | No, we actually just moved into this building six months ago. |
| Sanne | Well, it's really nice – very bright and airy. |
| J. María | Yes, it's a huge improvement on our previous building, that's for sure. |
| Sanne | How long has your company been around, anyway? I should probably know that, shouldn't I? |
| J. María | Well, the company was founded by Rafael Salas ten years ago. He was a very successful product designer for the American company IDEO, and he wanted to start something similar here in Spain. |
| Sanne | Ah, OK. And how many people are in the company now? I only know the team I work with – you know, you, Mary, Greg, and the others. But it looks like there are quite a few people here. |
| J. María | Yes, we've really expanded over the last few years – in contrast to most Spanish companies, I suppose. We currently have 31 employees and about seven different nationalities. |
| Sanne | Very international! And that's a good number. Not too small, but you still know everyone, I suppose. |
| J. María | Exactly. I'm very happy working here. So, Sanne, before we meet the others, would you like something to drink? Tea, coffee, water, juice ...? |
| Sanne | A cup of coffee would be great. I had an early start this morning. |
| J. María | No problem. How do you take it? Milk, sugar ...? |
| Sanne | Just black, thanks. |

## UNIT 2, EXERCISE 4

| | |
|---|---|
| Carl | Kathrin, hi. Nice to see you again. |
| Kathrin | Hi, Carl. Nice to see you too. Thanks for coming down to meet me. |
| Carl | Always a pleasure! Actually, after the restructuring last year we all got moved around, so I wasn't sure you'd be able to find my office by yourself. |
| Kathrin | Oh, really? Where are you now? |
| Carl | On the fourth floor. They decided to put sales and marketing together – at last! |
| Kathrin | That does make more sense, doesn't it? And the reception area looks very nice. |
| Carl | Yes, they finally repainted it in June. ... Oh, here's the lift now. After you. ... Was the driver there to meet you at the airport? |
| Kathrin | Yes, she was. Thanks so much for arranging that. |
| Carl | It's the least I could do after your early start! You must be exhausted now. |
| Kathrin | Oh, I'm all right. I managed to get some sleep, actually. |
| Carl | Here we are ... . So, can I get you something to drink? How about a cup of that tea you like so much? |
| Kathrin | That would be wonderful. And maybe a glass of water too? |
| Carl | Coming right up. ... Here you are. |
| Kathrin | Oh, thank you. |
| Carl | You're welcome. |
| Kathrin | Mm. You just don't get tea like this in Austria! |

## UNIT 2, EXERCISE 7

| | |
|---|---|
| Carl | Oh, Kathrin, would you mind waiting in my office for a few minutes? I just need to speak to a colleague before he leaves for Manchester this afternoon. |
| Kathrin | No problem, Carl. But where is your office now? |
| Carl | Oh, of course, you haven't been there yet. It's just down the corridor, the third door on the left. But come with me and I'll show you where it is. |
| Kathrin | Great. I'll just leave my bag here, if that's OK with you. But actually, I thought maybe I could just pop by Roger's office and say hello. |
| Carl | Oh, yeah. I'm sure he'd like to see you. |
| Kathrin | Where is he? |
| Carl | On the third floor. So, go out of the door and turn left to get into the lift. Then when you come out of the lift, go right, and it's the first door on your left. His name is on the door. |
| Kathrin | Great. So, I'll meet you back here in about ten minutes? |
| Carl | Sounds good. See you soon! |

## UNIT 2, EXERCISE 10

| | |
|---|---|
| J. María | All right, well, the first person I'd like you to meet is Valérie Dufour. She's our marketing manager. Valérie, this is Sanne Heitink. |
| Sanne | It's a pleasure to meet you, Valérie. |
| Valérie | Nice to meet you too. |
| J. María | And this is Mary Chan, our product designer. Have the two of you met before? |
| Sanne | No, we haven't actually, but we've exchanged a lot of emails. |
| Mary | It's great to finally meet you. It's nice to put a face to a name, isn't it? |
| Sanne | It certainly is. By the way, I really liked the prototype you sent us for the new gauge. |
| Mary | Oh, I'm glad to hear that. We're very happy with it, too. |
| J. María | Yes, Mary's got a great team working with her. |
| Mary | I know. I'm very lucky. Talking of which, this is my assistant, Greg Sánchez– I think you've had contact with him, haven't you? |
| Sanne | Ah, nice to meet you, Greg. I'm always sending you faxes, aren't I? |
| Greg | That's right. Good to meet you, Ms Heitink. |
| Sanne | Please, call me Sanne. Sorry about the mix-up with the specifications, by the way. We had a bit of a crisis back in Leiden ... |
| Greg | No problem. I'm just glad everything worked out. |
| J. María | And finally, this is Emin Murat, our sales manager for Turkey and the Middle East. |
| Sanne | I'm sorry, I didn't quite catch that. |
| Emin | Emin. Nice to meet you, Sanne. |
| Sanne | Nice to meet you too. |
| J. María | Well, I won't ask you to remember all of that. But you'll have a chance to get to know everyone better later. |
| Sanne | Sounds good. I'm afraid I'm not very good with names. |
| J. María | I know what you mean. So, shall we get some lunch? |
| Sanne | Sounds even better! |

## UNIT 3, EXERCISE 1

| | | |
|---|---|---|
| | Mary | Sorry, Sanne, it always takes a few minutes for everyone to arrive. |
| | Sanne | Not to worry. Is Anja still with the company, by the way? I didn't see her when José María was showing me around. |
| | Mary | She's not, actually. She left last July. As a matter of fact she's in Utrecht now. That's near you, isn't it? |
| | Sanne | It's not too far. Interesting … I should send her an email. Do you know what she's doing there? |
| | Mary | She's working as a designer for a bicycle manufacturer. I heard from her a couple of weeks ago, and she says things are going well. |
| | Sanne | That's good to hear. Actually, she did say she wanted to move closer to the sea one day. She enjoys sailing, doesn't she? |
| | Mary | That's right. She took us all out on her boat the weekend before she left. It was a lot of fun. |
| | Sanne | I can imagine. |
| | Mary | What about Chris? How's he doing these days? |
| | Sanne | He's doing fine. He says hello, by the way. He was promoted to product manager recently, so he's in the office more these days. |
| | Mary | Ah, that explains why I never see him at the trade fairs any more! |
| | J. María | Hi, everyone, sorry I'm a bit late. Just needed to gather some files for our meeting. So, if everyone would like to take a copy of today's agenda … |

## UNIT 3, EXERCISE 8

**Conversation 1**

| | | |
|---|---|---|
| | J. María | So, shall we start again at, say, 3.30? |
| | Sanne | Sounds good. |
| | Mary | Fine by me. Can I get you a coffee, Sanne? |
| | Sanne | Yes, that would be great, thanks, Mary. Can I just use the ladies' room first, though? |
| | Mary | Sorry? |
| | Sanne | Can I use your toilet? |
| | Mary | Oh, of course. It's just down the corridor, second door on the left. |
| | Sanne | Great, thanks. |

**Conversation 2**

| | | |
|---|---|---|
| | Mary | Here's your coffee. Just black, right? |
| | Sanne | That's right, thanks. That's an interesting painting you've got there, José María. |
| | J. María | Yes, a friend of mine did it. |
| | Sanne | Really? It's very colourful. |
| | J. María | That's his speciality. He's quite well known here in the area. |
| | Sanne | Does he do smaller ones as well? It's my husband's birthday next month and I know he would like his style. |
| | J. María | Sure, I can give you his phone number if you like. Just wait a second while I try to find it … |

**Conversation 3**

| | | |
|---|---|---|
| | Valérie | So Sanne, is this your first time in Spain? |
| | Sanne | Actually, no, I've been here a few times. |
| | Valérie | Oh really? Was that for business or pleasure? |
| | Sanne | Both. At my old company we did a lot of business with a firm in Barcelona, so I went over there a few times. And I've been to San Sebastian a couple of times. |

| | | |
|---|---|---|
| | Valérie | As a tourist? |
| | Sanne | Yes, to the jazz festival. My husband and I are huge jazz fans. |
| | Valérie | That's interesting. |
| | Sanne | What about you? Have you ever been to the Netherlands? |
| | Valérie | Just once, when I was a teenager. I did a school trip to Amsterdam. |
| | Sanne | Uh huh. And did you like it? |
| | Valérie | Yes, I loved it. Especially all the canals and cafés. |

## UNIT 4, EXERCISE 1

**Conversation 1**

| | | |
|---|---|---|
| | Jessica | And then this is the cathedral here. This kind of architecture is typical of our region. |
| | Phillip | Wow. It's really impressive. How old is it? |
| | Jessica | Oh, I should know that … I think it's from the 15th century but I'm not totally sure. We can go inside and check if you like? |
| | Phillip | Oh, it's not so important. I mean, it might be nice to … |

**Conversation 2**

| | | |
|---|---|---|
| | Rolf | That's the castle I was telling you about earlier. It was built by King Heinrich the Second. In German it's called a 'Schloss'. |
| | Phillip | Ah, that's what 'Schloss' means. I saw it on a sign back there. It really is beautiful. |
| | Rolf | Well, actually it was almost completely destroyed by bombing in the war and then rebuilt in the 1960s. So it's not all as old as it looks. |
| | Phillip | It's terrible how many historic buildings were damaged in the war. |
| | Rolf | Oh, that was all a long time ago … |

**Conversation 3**

| | | |
|---|---|---|
| | Jessica | Now this is something we're really proud of. It's our town's new art gallery. |
| | Phillip | My goodness. I've never seen a building like that before. |
| | Jessica | It was designed by the American architect Renzo Kindeslieb. Part of the building used to be a brewery. Brewing used to be a big industry here in Schwarzburg. |
| | Phillip | Really? Do they still make beer here? |
| | Jessica | Not any more. The brewery shut in 1992 after reunification. Anyway, the building is supposed to look like a beer bottle. |
| | Phillip | Oh yes, I see that now. |
| | Jessica | It's good, isn't it? He actually won a prize for it. |
| | Phillip | I don't understand why it doesn't fall over. |
| | Jessica | Neither do I. It's amazing, isn't it? |

## UNIT 4, EXERCISE 6

| | | |
|---|---|---|
| | Sharon | So are you both from Modena originally? |
| | Mauro | I am, but Cristina is from Milano. |
| | Cristina | Well, a little village about 60km from Milano actually. But I normally say I'm from Milano because it's easier. |
| | Sharon | Ah, OK. So how long have you lived here? |
| | Cristina | Seven years. I went to university in Torino and then when I graduated I moved to Modena because of my boyfriend. He's from here. |
| | Sharon | And do you like living here? |

| | |
|---|---|
| Cristina | I do. I mean, it's maybe a bit on the small side and there's not much nightlife, but the quality of life is really good here. And it's really nice that you can be out in the countryside in just thirty minutes. |
| Sharon | Yeah, that's something I miss working in a city. I grew up on a farm, so I miss the countryside sometimes. |
| Cristina | Interesting. Well, if we have time, perhaps we can drive out into the country. It's really beautiful. |
| Sharon | That would be nice. I've actually got the afternoon free tomorrow and I was wondering if you had any recommendations for things to do. |
| Mauro | There's a fantastic car museum at Panzano, which is not far from here. It's in a beautiful castle. I can take you if you like. |
| Sharon | Well, that's very kind of you, but my flight's at 6 p.m. so I should probably stay in town just to make sure I get to the airport in time. |
| Cristina | I know what you can do. The antique fair is on tomorrow. There are about two hundred stands. It's really good. |
| Sharon | That sounds great. I love antiques. Where is it exactly? |
| Cristina | Parco Novi Sud. I'll take you if you want. |
| Sharon | Well, if it's no trouble … |
| Cristina | None at all. I'll pick you up at the hotel. Say ten? |

## UNIT 4, EXERCISE 11

**🔊 19**

**Conversation 1**
A   I was wondering if you would like to join us for dinner tonight?
B   That sounds really nice. Thanks very much.

**🔊 20**

**Conversation 2**
A   How about meeting for a coffee next week?
B   I'd love to, but I'm actually away at a trade fair all next week. How about the week after that?

**🔊 21**

**Conversation 3**
A   I have an extra ticket for the opera tonight. Would you like to come?
B   That's very kind of you, but I'm meeting a friend for dinner this evening. Maybe you can let me know next time you're going?

**🔊 22**

**Conversation 4**
A   My partner and I are having a party next Saturday. We were hoping you could come.
B   Thanks, I'd like that very much.

## UNIT 5, EXERCISE 1

**🔊 23**

| | |
|---|---|
| Anna | This looks a really nice place. |
| Bruno | I hope you like it, Anna. We come here quite often with visitors. It's very typical. Are you hungry? |
| Anna | Well, I got up early this morning and I only had a tiny sandwich on the plane. |
| Bruno | So? |
| Anna | I'm absolutely starving. |
| Bruno | I'm afraid they don't have menus in English here, but just say if you need help with anything. |
| Anna | OK. How many courses are we having, Carlo? |
| Carlo | A starter and a main course then we can decide later about dessert. |

| | |
|---|---|
| Anna | That's fine with me. Where are the starters? |
| Carlo | They're here, then these are fish dishes, and the meat ones are on the next page. |
| Anna | What do you recommend? |
| Bruno | Everything is good. |
| Anna | What's this? |
| Bruno | That's mushrooms in a cream sauce. |
| Carlo | I'm having that. Followed by the tuna. It comes with asparagus and small potatoes roasted in the oven. |
| Anna | That sounds great. I'll have the same. With a salad instead of the potatoes. What about you Bruno? |
| Bruno | I'll have the soup followed by the pasta. I don't eat much meat these days. |
| Anna | Is that for health reasons? |
| Bruno | Yes, my wife thinks I should lose a little weight. She's probably right. What would you like to drink? |
| Anna | White wine? And maybe some water? |
| Carlo | Just the water for me, Bruno. I'm driving. I thought I could show you the old town and the cathedral later. |
| Anna | That would be lovely. |
| Bruno | Well, I'm not driving, so I'll share a bottle of white with Anna. You can choose the water, Carlo. |
| Carlo | OK, Sparkling in that case. Right. Let's see if we can catch the waiter's attention. |

## UNIT 5, EXERCISE 6

**🔊 24**

| | |
|---|---|
| Bruno | So, how did you like the tuna, Anna? |
| Anna | Oh, it was very tasty and perfectly cooked. How was your pasta? |
| Bruno | Very nice indeed. The sauce was wonderful. And just the right amount. |
| Carlo | Would anybody like dessert? |
| Bruno | Let's wait a bit, shall we? |
| Anna | Good idea. So do you come here often? |
| Carlo | Usually when I have guests. It's a bit rich for every day. |
| Anna | What about you, Bruno? |
| Bruno | I used to eat here a lot when I worked in this part of town but as I said my wife is trying to get me to eat better these days. |
| Anna | So are you married as well, Carlo? You mentioned your mother-in-law earlier. |
| Carlo | Yes, I just got married last year actually. We had a great honeymoon in Croatia. |
| Anna | Really? We went to Croatia last summer for our holiday. It's gorgeous isn't it? |
| Carlo | It certainly is. We played tennis nearly every day. It was great. Do you do any sports, Anna? |
| Anna | Just jogging. Can I run anywhere here? |
| Bruno | Yes, there is a lovely run from your hotel through the woods down to the old town and back. I'll show you later. |
| Anna | Thanks. |
| Carlo | You were saying you went to Croatia last year. Where else have you been? |
| Anna | Greece, Turkey, France. Talking of France, I've still got room for dessert. Let's look at the menu shall we? |

## UNIT 5, EXERCISE 12

25

| | |
|---|---|
| Anna | Well I don't know about you two, but I'm ready to hit the hay. |
| Bruno | Sorry? |
| Anna | You know, I'm tired, ready for bed. |
| Bruno | Me too. It's been a long day. |
| Carlo | Does anyone want a coffee? |
| Anna | No thanks. |
| Bruno | Me neither. |
| Carlo | I'll get one with the bill. Let me try and catch the waiter. Excuse me? Can I have a black coffee and the bill, please?..... |
| Anna | Let me get this. |
| Carlo | No, it's OK I'll get it. You're our guest. |
| Anna | Seriously, it's on me. You have paid for everything all day. I'm going to put it on expenses any way. |
| Bruno | Well, that's very kind. |
| Carlo | Yes, very generous. |
| Anna | You're very welcome. Now, the waiter was great. How much can I tip him? |
| Carlo | Just round up the total and add 10%. Tell him to keep the change. |
| Anna | But I'm paying by card. |
| Bruno | In here? Unlikely. |
| Anna | But I don't have any cash on me! |
| Bruno | Maybe we should pay after all. They only take cash ... |

## UNIT 6, EXERCISE 2

### Conversation 1

26

| | |
|---|---|
| Ute | I'm sorry, but I couldn't help noticing you've got a Chipper bag. Do you work for them? |
| Lloyd | No, actually, they're one of our suppliers. |
| Ute | What a coincidence – they're one of our suppliers too. I'm Ute Adena, by the way. |
| Lloyd | Lloyd Roberts. Nice to meet you. So, Ute, what company are you with? |
| Ute | I'm the head of purchasing at Pixdorf. We make software for retail POS systems. |
| Lloyd | Oh yes, I've heard of your company before. Am I right in thinking you're based in Frankfurt? |
| Ute | Yes. Well, just outside Frankfurt actually, in a little place called Bad Homburg. |
| Lloyd | Right. |
| Ute | And who do you work for? |
| Lloyd | I work in the purchasing department of a small company called Specialized Solutions in Birmingham. |
| Ute | Right. I don't think I've come across them before. |
| Lloyd | So I assume you're here for the trade fair? |
| Ute | Yes, exactly. |
| Lloyd | This is quite a nice hotel, isn't it? |
| Ute | Oh, it is. The breakfast this morning was delicious. |

### Conversation 2

27

| | |
|---|---|
| Ute | Excuse me, do you know if this is the stop for the CASPA trade fair? |
| Yves | Yes, it is. The next bus should be arriving in five minutes. |
| Ute | Great. What a beautiful day! |
| Yves | Yes, it is, isn't it? In France it was raining all last week, so this is a nice change. |
| Ute | I know. I'm from Germany, near Frankfurt, and it was actually snowing when I left. |
| Yves | Ugh! ... So, are you looking after a stand at the fair? |
| Ute | No, I'm actually just here to look around and do some networking, you know. What about you? |
| Yves | We have a stand here. I'm with a French company called Plein Air, and we're introducing new inventory software. |
| Ute | Oh, that sounds interesting. Where are you based? |
| Yves | In Toulouse. Do you know it? |
| Ute | Oh, yes. I visited Toulouse and the area last summer, actually. It's a wonderful part of France. Airbus has its headquarters there, right? |
| Yves | That's right. It's the backbone of the city's industrial base, in fact the whole region's. And what about you? What do you do? |
| Ute | I'm the head of purchasing at Pixdorf. |
| Yves | And that's near Frankfurt, you said? |
| Ute | Exactly – Bad Homburg. Have you ever been to Germany? |
| Yves | Only once, on a school exchange. I keep meaning to visit, though. Ah, here's our bus! |
| Ute | Great. |
| Yves | Please, after you ... |

### Conversation 3

28

| | |
|---|---|
| Ute | Excuse me, do you mind if I join you? |
| Per | Not at all. |
| Ute | I'm Ute Adena. |
| Per | Nice to meet you. I'm Per Jensen. |
| Ute | Nice to meet you too. ... Do you know if it's table service here, or do we have to go to the counter? |
| Per | It's table service. So you can sit back and relax! |
| Ute | Yeah, I really need a break. So, when did you get here? |
| Per | On Monday. And you? |
| Ute | Just today, actually. So, what do you think of the fair so far? |
| Per | It's quite good. Certainly better than last year. |
| Ute | Have you seen anything interesting? |
| Per | Well, one company has developed a really nice security device for clothing. It's very secure, but doesn't damage clothing the way current tags do. That's always a real headache for us. |
| Ute | Really? That sounds like something worth checking out. |
| Per | Well, if you want to take a look, just go to section B. The stand is right near the door. |
| Ute | Thanks for the tip! |

## UNIT 6, EXERCISE 6

29

| | |
|---|---|
| Thomas | So you see we really have some very exciting new products. |
| Ute | They're certainly very interesting. Anyway, let me give you my card. |
| Thomas | Thank you. Now, I absolutely have to show you our new wireless printer. Let me just get it for you ... |
| Ute | Listen, that's very kind of you but I should probably get going. |
| Thomas | It'll only take a minute. It's really one of our most interesting developments. |

Ute    I'd love to see it, but I should really get going. I'm actually supposed to be meeting someone in ten minutes.

Thomas    Oh, I'm sure they won't mind if you're a couple of minutes late …

Ute    Why don't I come back afterwards to take a look?

Thomas    Well, if you're sure you don't have time.

Ute    No, I'm afraid I really should go. I'll come right back after my appointment.

Thomas    Great. I'll be here.

Ute    See you in a little while, then.

Thomas    See you later.

## UNIT 6, EXERCISE 10

**30**  **a** Oh no, it's the last day of the fair and I've only managed to hand out three business cards. That means I've got to get rid of 197 today or my boss'll kill me! Perhaps I'll just give one to everyone on the plane back tonight!

**31**  **b** Look at this amazing pen I got at the Sony stand. It's also a voice recorder. I can't believe they give away such cool stuff these days.

**32**  **c** It always amazes me at trade fairs how people carry around these ugly free bags. They're wearing their best thousand-euro suits but they have these one-euro bags they've got from the sponsor. Isn't that weird?

**33**  **d** I had this really strange experience earlier today. I was in the bathroom washing my hands, and this guy comes up to me and tries to give me his business card. In the bathroom! Can you imagine?

**34**  **e** This is really the worst-organized trade fair I've ever seen. My five-year-old son could do a better job of running it.

**35**  **f** I'm sorry I keep looking at my phone. My daughter is ill today and my husband is at home looking after her. I'm waiting for him to call me to tell me how she is. I hate being away from home when my kids are ill.

## UNIT 6, OUTPUT

**36**  **A** That reminds me of a trip I made to Paris last year. It was a complete nightmare. I got to Heathrow around four to find my flight is cancelled and all other flights are full. I have to go because I have a really important meeting, so I get a taxi down to London and jump on the Eurostar. Just outside London, the train grinds to a halt and we stay there for about two hours. Everyone rushes to the buffet car and all the food goes within about an hour. I'm right at the back of the queue and get nothing. I finally get to Paris just after midnight and grab a cab. The driver looks at me strangely wondering why I am out so late. He takes ages finding the hotel and we finally stop outside a very dark Hotel California, honestly that's the name! The driver races off and I ring the bell and wait. I ring the bell. I wait. Finally, after an age, the door is opened by a young guy who looks half-asleep. No chance of dinner, everything in the area is closed. Oh well … just give me my bed. The lift is broken so I walk up to the fourth floor. I open the door and scream because there, right in the middle of a pure white bedspread is … the largest spider you've ever seen!

# Useful phrases and vocabulary

## MEETING SOMEONE ON ARRIVAL

### Greeting a visitor

Hello, I'm Kasia Janiak from BTO Systems.

You must be Raj. Welcome to London.

Nice/Good to see you again. *(when you know sb already)*

– Good to see you too.

It's a pleasure to meet you (at last)./It's great to finally meet you in person. *(meeting sb for the first time)*

– It's a pleasure/Nice/Good/Great to meet you too.

Please, call me Sanne.

– And I'm José María, of course.

### Apologizing for a delay

I hope you haven't been waiting long.

– Don't worry. I just got here ten minutes ago.

Sorry to keep you waiting. The train was on time but the traffic here is terrible.

– No problem. I know how it is.

Sorry I'm late. My flight was delayed because of bad weather.

### Asking about the journey

How was the/your flight/journey/drive?

– Uneventful, thankfully./Fine, thanks.

– Not so good. The traffic was terrible.

– OK, but there was some turbulence.

You must be exhausted now.

– Oh, I'm OK. I managed to get some sleep, actually.

– I am a bit tired, I have to say.

### Offering and accepting help

Can I help you with your bags?/Do you need a hand/any help with that?/Shall I take that for you?

– That would be great/very nice, thanks.

Would you mind taking this?

– Not at all./Of course not.

Let me get that for you.

### Freshening up

I'd just like to wash my hands (if that's OK/before we get going).

Is there a toilet (BrE)/bathroom/restroom (AmE) around here/somewhere?

– Yes, there's one just this way …

Is there a café where we could sit down/get something to drink?

– Yes, there's a nice one just over there.

– I'm not sure, but let's see if we can find one.

Do you mind if we grab/get a quick coffee before we get going?

– Not at all.

– Actually we're in a little bit of a hurry. Maybe we could have one later?

## Taking the visitor to their hotel or the company

So, if you'll just come this way …

The/My car is parked over here.

We can get a taxi over there.

Where are we going from here?

– I thought we could go to the hotel first.

– We should probably go straight to the office, if that's OK.

– I'll take you to your hotel.

Is the hotel/office/conference centre far from here?

– No, it's just 15 minutes away.

– It's probably about a 30-minute drive, but we have plenty of time.

### Talking about plans and schedules

It's not far now./We'll be there in five minutes.

I thought you might like to check into your hotel first and drop off your things.

– Sounds good./Sure.

Would you like to check into your hotel first?

– Actually, we can go straight to the office if you prefer.

Then we can grab/get a spot of lunch.

There's a nice Italian place near your hotel.

After that we can go to the company.

We have the meeting with the sales team at two, as you know.

At four we're going to visit the production plant.

That should only take an hour.

Then I'll take you back to your hotel and you can relax for a bit.

I'll pick you up at about seven for dinner.

We're going to a very nice restaurant this evening.

– Sounds good./Great.

## LOOKING AFTER A VISITOR TO YOUR COMPANY

### Welcoming a visitor

Hello, Ms Heitink. I'm José María Molinero.

Nice to meet you/see you again.

Welcome to Salas Design/our company.

Did you have any trouble finding us?

– No, not at all. The directions on your website/Your directions were very clear/good.

Was the driver there to meet you at the airport?

– Yes, he/she was. Thanks so much for arranging that.

– It's the least I could do (after your long flight).

Thanks for coming down to meet me.

– No problem at all. I wasn't sure you'd be able to find my office by yourself.

### Showing a visitor around your offices

You can leave your things/your briefcase/coat here/in my office/at the reception desk.

Would you like to leave your things here?

– That would be nice, thanks.

I'll just leave my bag here, if that's OK with you.
I'll take you round to meet a few members of the team.
They're all looking forward to meeting you.
Would you mind waiting in my office for a few minutes?
– Not at all./Sure, no problem.
I just need to make some copies before the meeting.
I thought maybe I could just pop by Roger's office and say hello.
Can/Could I use your bathroom (AmE)?
– Of course. I'll just show you where it is.
If you'll just come this way …
Here's the lift now.
After you. *(when entering a lift or going through a door)*

### Offering a guest something to eat or drink
Would you like something to drink? Tea, coffee, water …?
So, can I get you something to drink?
– A cup of coffee would be great.
– Just a glass of water, thanks.
– I'm OK for the moment, thanks.
Can I get you a coffee?/How about a cup of tea?
– That would be great/wonderful. Thanks very much.
How do you take your coffee?/How would you like that?
– Just black, thanks.
– With milk/cream (AmE), please.
– Milk and sugar, please.
Could I have a glass of water as well, please?
– Coming right up./Of course.
Here you are./Here's your coffee. *(giving a drink)*
Thank you.
– You're welcome./No problem.
– Not at all./Don't mention it.
Shall we get some lunch?
– Sounds good. It's been a long time since breakfast.
– Maybe I'll just have a coffee. I'm not actually that hungry.

### Giving directions
Where are you now?/Where is your office now?
– On the fourth floor./Just down here.
Which floor is your office on?
– The eighth! Don't worry – we'll take the lift/elevator (AmE).
Where is the toilet/bathroom (AmE)/Mike's office?
It's just down the hall/round the corner on the left/right.
It's the first/second/third door on the left/right.
It's next to the toilet/front door/kitchen.
Just go out of the door and turn left to get to the lift.
– That's very clear, thanks./Thanks, I'm sure I'll find it.
– Sorry, could you explain that again?
Come with me and I'll show you where it is!
I'll meet you back here in ten minutes, OK?
– Sounds good. See you soon!

### Introducing a visitor to your colleagues
The first person I'd like you to meet is Valérie Dufour.
She's our marketing manager.
Valérie, this is Sanne Heitink.
– It's a pleasure to meet you, Sanne./It's great to finally meet you.

– Nice to meet you too.
And this is Mary Chan, our product designer.
I'd like to introduce Mr Sánchez. He's the new head of production.
Have the two of you met before?
– No, we haven't, but we've exchanged a lot of emails.
– Yes, (I think) we actually met once at a trade fair.
It's nice to put a name to a face, isn't it?
– It certainly is.
I think you've had contact with her.
She'll be your contact person on the IT side of the project.
You'll have a chance to get to know everyone a bit better at this afternoon's meeting.
I'm afraid I'm not very good with names.
– I know what you mean!

### At a meeting
Sorry, it always takes a few minutes for everyone to arrive.
– Not to worry./No problem.
Hi, everyone, sorry I'm a bit late. I just needed to gather some files for our meeting.
So, if everyone would like to take a copy of today's agenda …
Well, I suppose we should make a start.
So, shall we get down to business?
Right, let's make a start, shall we?
So, shall we start again at, say, 3.30? *(before a break)*
– Sounds good.

## ENTERTAINING A VISITOR

### Showing a visitor around your town or city
This is the old town square/cathedral (here).
Let me show you the museum/town hall.
This kind of architecture is typical of our region.
That's the castle I was telling you about earlier.
It was built/designed by …
It's really impressive/beautiful.
I've never seen a building like this before.
How old is it?
– I think it's from the 15th century but I'm not totally sure.

### Asking for/Giving recommendations for sightseeing
I've actually got the afternoon free tomorrow.
I was wondering if you had any recommendations for things to do.
I know what you can do.
There's a(n) great/fantastic/interesting art gallery/shop/park/street.
There's a nice exhibition of photos on at the town hall at the moment.
There's a fantastic art gallery just an hour from here.
If we have time we can maybe show you one of the lakes nearby.
– That would be nice./Sounds great.
It's/They're very interesting/beautiful/amazing.
I can take you if you like.
It's really/definitely worth visiting/seeing/a visit.
I'd really like to do that./I'd love to see that.

### Asking for/Giving directions in a town or city

Where is the town hall/station/museum exactly?
How do I get there?/What's the best way to get there?
It's next to/near/just around the corner from/on the
    same street as your hotel/the town hall/square.
Just go along this street, then turn left/right.
Take the second/third street on the left/right.
Keep going until you see the church/bank.
You can walk there from here.

### Invitations

*Making an invitation*
I was wondering if you might like to join us for dinner
    tonight?
How about meeting for a coffee next week?
I have a spare ticket for the opera tonight. Would you
    like to come?
My partner and I are having a party next Saturday. We
    were hoping you could come.

*Accepting an invitation*
That sounds really nice/great. Thanks very much.
Thanks, I'd like that very much.
That would be lovely.
Good idea. Let's do that.

*Turning down an invitation*
I'd love to, but I'm actually away at a trade fair all next
    week.
That's very kind of you, but I'm supposed to be meeting
    a friend for dinner this evening.
I'd love to come, but I'm afraid I just don't have time
    today.

*Making an alternative suggestion*
How about the week after that?
Maybe you can let me know next time you're going?
Maybe we could go for dinner tomorrow instead?
How about having lunch sometime next week?

#### EATING OUT

### Restaurant small talk

This looks a really nice place.
It's very typical.
I'm a bit hungry/absolutely starving.
Do you come here often?
– Oh yes. I was here last week actually.
– Usually when I have guests.
I used to eat here a lot when I worked in this part of
    town.
What do you recommend?

### Helping with the menu

I'm afraid they don't have English menus here.
Just say if you need help with anything.
I might need help with some of this.
Is that some kind of meat?
So what's …?
– It's a kind of fish/meat/vegetable/pasta/ dumpling.
– It's (a bit) like an omelette.
– It's made with eggs, milk and sugar.
– It's a local speciality.
– It's typical of/a speciality of our region.
– It's a spicy/savoury/sweet dish.
– It's made with meat/fish/vegetables.
You have to try that/those.

### Ordering

Do you know what you're having?
Have you decided yet?
– Yes. I think I'll have the steak.
– I'm still trying to make up my mind. It all looks so
    good.
– I think I need a couple more minutes, if that's OK.
(I think) I'll have that for my main course (then).
I'm going to have the special.
Let's see if we can catch the waiter's attention.
I'd like/I'll have the pasta, please. *(to the waiter)*
Have you still got room for dessert?

### Paying for the meal

Shall we get the bill?
I'll see if I can catch the waiter when he goes past.
Can we have the bill, please? *(to the waiter)*
Could you bring us the bill, please?
Let me get this./This is on me./I'll get this.
– No, it's OK. I'll get it.
– Are you sure? That's very kind/generous of you.
That was lovely, thank you./Thanks for the meal. It was
    really nice.
– You're very welcome.
– It was my/a pleasure.
What do I do about tipping?
– You just round up the total.
– I normally leave … per cent.
I don't have any cash on me.
Do they accept credit cards here?

#### AT A TRADE FAIR

### Starting a conversation with a stranger

I'm sorry, but I couldn't help noticing you've got a
    Chipper bag. Do you work for them?
Excuse me, do you know if this is the stop for the trade
    fair?
Excuse me, do you mind if I join you?
– Not at all.
Are you here for the trade fair?
– Yes, exactly.
I'm Ute Adena, by the way.
– Lloyd Roberts. Nice to meet you.

### Talking about the trade fair

Are you looking after a stand at the fair?
– Yes, we have a stand here.
– I'm actually just here to look around and do some networking.
When did you get here?
– On Wednesday./Just today, actually.
So, what do you think of the fair so far?
– I'm enjoying it a lot.
– It's quite good. Certainly better than last year.
– I'm a bit disappointed, to tell the truth.
Have you seen anything interesting?
– Yes, one company has developed a really nice …/ some interesting new …
– Not really, to be honest.
That sounds like something worth checking out.
If you want to take a look, just go to section/hall B.
The stand is right near the door.
Thanks for the tip!

### Talking about your company

What company are you with?
– I'm the head of purchasing at Pixdorf.
– I'm with a French company called Plein Air.
And what about you? What do you do?
And who do you work for?
What does your company do (exactly)?
– We make software for retail POS systems.
I've heard of your company before. Where are you based?
– In Toulouse. Do you know it?
Am I right in thinking you're based in Frankfurt?
– Yes, that's right.
– Well, just outside Frankfurt actually.

### Talking to a person at a stand

So you see we really have some very exciting new products/services.
It's really one of our most interesting developments.
I absolutely have to show you/demonstrate our new …
It'll only take a minute.
It's/They're certainly very interesting.

### Ending a conversation

Anyway, let me give you my card.
Listen, do you have a card?
Why don't I come back afterwards to take a look?
Sorry, I really have to go now.
I should really get going. I have another appointment in a couple of minutes.
I'm actually supposed to be meeting someone in ten minutes.
Listen, I've just seen Chris over there. Excuse me a moment, I really need to catch him.

### MISCELLANEOUS COMMUNICATION SKILLS

### Reacting to what someone says

That must be very stressful/an interesting job.
You must be very proud of her.
That must have been very exciting/nice.
That must have been a difficult time for you.

### Asking for clarification

(I'm) sorry, I didn't quite catch that.
(I'm) sorry, could you tell me your name again?
Sorry, could you say that for me again?
I'm sorry, I don't quite follow you.
I'm not totally sure what you mean.
Did you say 15 or 50?

### Keeping a conversation going

Have you ever been to Hong Kong?
– No, I haven't. What about you?
– Yes, I have. I was there two years ago on business.
This is actually my second visit.
– Oh really? When were you here before?

### SMALL TALK

### Talking about the weather

How was the weather when you left?
– It was raining, as usual!/It was very nice, actually.
I can't believe it's so sunny/hot/cold here.
What a beautiful day!
– It is, isn't it?
It was actually snowing when I left home.
This summer/winter has been terrible/OK/lovely/great.
The last couple of weeks have been very warm/cold.
Do you normally get good summers here?
– Usually we get at least a few hot days, but sometimes it rains a lot.
– Not really!
I imagine the winters here must be pretty cold.
– Oh yes. Sometimes it goes down to minus 15.
– Actually they're not as cold as you might think.

### Talking about travel

Is this your first time here?
– Actually, no, I've been here a few times.
– Actually, I was here once before, in 2001.
– Yes it is. I'm really enjoying it.
Have you been here before?
– No, this is my first time.
– Yes, I've been here a couple of times.
When were you here before?
– I was here two years ago/in 2005.
Have you ever been to England?
– Just once, when I was a teenager. I did a school exchange to London.
– No, never. I've always wanted to go there.
Was that for business or pleasure?
– It was a business trip.
– I was just there on holiday. It was very relaxing!
– A bit of both.
Did you enjoy your visit to …?

– Yes, very much. Especially the food!
– It was OK, but the weather wasn't so great.
What did you think of ...?
– It's an amazing city. Pity about the weather though!
Where did you stay when you were there?
– We found this fantastic hotel right next to the river.

## Talking about a company's offices

This is a lovely space you have here.
It's a really nice building – very bright and airy.
It's a huge improvement on our previous building.
To be honest, I liked the old building better.
It's a great neighbourhood – lots of green space and some nice cafés.
The only problem is there are no restaurants nearby/it's difficult to park here.
Have you been in this location long?
– No, we actually just moved into this building six months ago.
– Yes, we've been here for more than ten years.

## Talking about a company

How long has your company been around?
– It was founded by Rafael Salas ten years ago.
– We've been going for almost 50 years.
How many people are in the company now?
– We currently have 31 employees.
– We have about 200 staff at the moment.
We've really expanded over the last few years.

## Talking about mutual acquaintances

How's Marita these days?
What's Carol up to?
Have you heard anything from Josef recently?
What about Chris? How's he doing these days?
– He's doing fine.
Is Anja still with the company, by the way?
– She's not, actually. She left last July.
– Yes, she's still here.
As a matter of fact she's in Utrecht now.
Do you know what she's doing there?
I heard from him/her a couple of weeks ago.
He/She was promoted to product manager recently.
Is that Chris Bennett you're talking about?
– Exactly.
He/She says hello, by the way.
I should send him/her an email.
Say hi to Maria for me. (informal)
Give my regards to Maria. (neutral/formal)
Should I tell him/her hi from you?
– Could you? That would be nice.

## Talking about personal possessions

That's an interesting painting/picture/photograph you've got there.
I like that painting/picture/photograph. Where did you get it?
It's very colourful/beautiful/interesting/different.
I couldn't help noticing your new Blackberry.

## Talking about where you are from

Are you from Paris originally?
– Yes, I am.
– No, I'm actually from Brussels.
I'm actually from a little village just outside Rome.
I was born in Barcelona, but I grew up in Madrid.
I used to live in Krakow.
I went to university in Michigan.
I graduated from university in 1995.
Where did you live before that?
Did you go to college/university/vocational school in [name of town/city]?
What did you study?
Do you ever miss America?
– Yes, I do. Especially the food!
– Not really, but I do miss my family.
– Not at all! I'm very happy here.

## Talking about where you live

I live in/near/not far from ...
How long have you lived here?
Do you like living here?
It's maybe a bit on the small side.
The cultural life is really good.
There's a lot going on.
It's quite expensive to live here.
It's really nice that you can be out in the countryside in just thirty minutes.

## Talking about free-time activities

So, what do you like doing in your free time?
Do you have any hobbies?/Do you do any sports?
I love/like/don't like/hate cooking/reading.
I often go to the gym/play tennis/do yoga after work/at the weekend.
I like swimming/sailing/going to the theatre but I never have the time.
I try to play football/squash at least once a week.
If I had more time, I would go to more concerts/eat out more.

## Talking about family relationships

Are you married (as well)?
– Yes, I just got married last year, actually.
– No, I live with my partner.
– I'm actually single at the moment.
Let me show you some photos.
Do you have any brothers or sisters?
Is [name] married?
Does [name] have any children?
How old is [name]?
[Name] got married in 2002.
He/She has ... children.
They are married/separated/divorced.
He/She is ... years old.
My husband/wife is a meteorologist/an analyst.
My son/daughter has just got a place at university.

# Vocabulary banks

## THE WEATHER

| words describing weather in general | words describing temperature | words describing the sky | words to do with water | weather verbs |
|---|---|---|---|---|
| good | freezing | cloudy | wet | to rain |
| great | cold | grey | damp | to pour |
| fantastic | chilly | overcast | drizzling | to drizzle |
| lovely | mild | clear | humid | to freeze |
| OK | warm | sunny | pouring | to hail |
| changeable | hot | | rainy | to snow |
| depressing | boiling | | | to shine |
| miserable | roasting | | | to cloud over/to clear |
| terrible | | | | up (sky) |

## COMPANIES

| talking about the building | talking about the company structure | verbs to do with the history of the company or building | adjectives for rooms and buildings |
|---|---|---|---|
| location | employees | to found | bright |
| (first/second/third) floor | staff | to set up | sunny |
| reception (area) | personnel | to expand | airy |
| lift/elevator (AmE) | colleagues | to open a new office | light |
| stairs | department | to close an office/a department | dark |
| neighbourhood | division | to restructure | crowded |
| toilet/bathroom/restroom (AmE) | branch | to downsize | spacious |
| kitchen | subsidiary | to move (into/out of) | old |
| photocopier room | parent company | to take on new staff | modern |
| meeting/conference room | head office | to lay off staff | beautiful |
| car park | | | ugly |

| types of furniture and office equipment | company departments |
|---|---|
| (office) chair | administration |
| stool | book keeping/accounts |
| table | purchasing |
| desk | sales & marketing |
| reception desk | production |
| cupboard | legal |
| notice board | research & development (R&D) |
| whiteboard | logistics |
| flipchart | customer services |
| overhead projector | technical support |
| projector | IT |
| | human resources (HR) |

## FREE-TIME ACTIVITIES

| sport | relaxing at home | going out | hobbies and pastimes |
|---|---|---|---|
| playing football/squash/tennis/ golf | listening to music | eating out/going to restaurants | playing cards/board games |
| (going) sailing/swimming/ skiing/jogging/cycling/inline skating | reading | going to the cinema/theatre/ opera/museums/concerts/ pubs/bars | doing crosswords/ puzzles/Sudoku |
| | watching television | | |
| | cooking | (going) shopping | photography/ drawing/painting |
| keeping fit | visiting friends | going clubbing | DIY/home |
| going to the gym | doing nothing | meeting friends | improvements |
| doing yoga/karate/tai chi | | | |

## TOWNS AND CITIES

| places in a town/city | words to describe towns/cities | phrases to describe relative size and location |
|---|---|---|
| airport | beautiful | a bit bigger than |
| harbour | historic | much smaller than |
| railway station | important | about the same size as |
| bus station | industrial | (not that) close to |
| art gallery | thriving | near |
| museum | fashionable | right next to |
| castle | growing | part of |
| cathedral | large | on the (name of river) |
| mosque | small | not far from |
| synagogue | ancient | |
| park | old | |
| sports/leisure centre | modern | |
| swimming pool | cheap | |
| old town centre | expensive | |
| town/city hall | | |
| shopping centre/mall (AmE) | | |
| university | | |

## FOOD

| parts of the meal | types of meat | types of vegetable | side dishes | ways of cooking | describing food |
|---|---|---|---|---|---|
| aperitif | bacon | aubergine/ eggplant (AmE) | chips (BrE)/ French fries (AmE) | to bake | heavy |
| starter | beef | | | to fry | light |
| main course | chicken | pepper | potato wedges | to deep fry | rich |
| dessert/pudding (BrE) | ham | (red) cabbage | rice | to grill (BrE)/to broil (AmE) | savoury |
| digestif | lamb | courgette (BrE)/ zucchini (AmE) | salad | to roast | spicy |
| | pork | | noodles | to toast | sweet |
| | rabbit | onion | | to sauté | fatty |
| | veal | cucumber | | to microwave | fattening |
| | venison | lettuce | | | salty |
| | | sweetcorn | | | sugary |
| | | mushroom | | | tasty |
| | | turnip | | | delicious |
| | | parsnip | | | disgusting |

| dairy products | describing hunger |
|---|---|
| milk | hungry |
| cheese | peckish |
| yoghurt | starving |
| cream cheese | ravenous |
| | full |

## FAMILY AND RELATIONSHIPS

| words to describe marital status | words for talking about family members and friends | verbs connected to families and relationships |
|---|---|---|
| single | mother-in-law | to be born |
| engaged | father-in-law | to meet someone |
| married | brother-in-law | to make sb's acquaintance |
| separated | sister-in-law | to introduce sb to sb |
| divorced | step-daughter | to get to know sb |
| widowed | step-son | to get engaged |
| | only child | to get married |
| | ex-wife | to separate |
| | ex-husband | to get divorced |
| | best friend | to be pregnant |
| | acquaintance | to have a baby |
| | partner | |